Christianity and Child Sexual Abuse

Christianity and Child Sexual Abuse

Hilary Cashman

First published in Great Britain 1993
Society for Promoting Christian Knowledge
Holy Trinity Church
Marylebone Road
London NW1 4DU

British Library Cataloguing-in-Publication Data
A catalogue record for this book is available from the British Library

ISBN 0–281–04647–6

Typeset by Deltatype Ltd, Ellesmere Port
Printed in Great Britain by
Mackays of Chatham plc, Chatham, Kent

This book is dedicated to the 'wounded healers',
especially Margaret Kennedy and Sharon Gray.

Contents

Preface

I would like to thank the friends and colleagues who have helped me by contributing their experiences, comments and information; especially Sheila Briggs, Anne Borrowdale, Colin Carr, Marietta Higgs, Margaret Kennedy, Jim O'Keefe, Sue McKenzie, Diane, Joan, Ron, Sharon, Lyn, Emma; and members of Safety Net and Christian Survivors of Sexual Abuse. My respect for the integrity, wisdom and generosity of the abuse survivors I encountered while writing this book is beyond words. If I have written anything with which they disagree I hope it will be the basis for future fruitful discussion.

I am grateful to my husband Rob and my children Leila, Matty and Joe, for their love, support and tolerance.

Hilary Cashman

Introduction:
The disappeared

There is among the Queen's pictures a snow scene by Bruegel the Elder, showing soldiers entering a village. At first sight it is a typical Bruegel scene, busy, populous, detailed and picturesque. On closer inspection it becomes puzzling. These are not the happy village folk Bruegel usually shows us; they seem agitated, tearful and afraid, but it is not clear why. Some of them are holding bundles of washing, others are leading animals.

The painting was originally called 'The Massacre of the Innocents'. The bundles of washing and animals were originally murdered children, later changed or painted out, probably because the painting seemed to refer too directly to a contemporary atrocity perpetrated by Spanish troops in a Netherlands town, and political caution impelled its transformation to a harmless village scene. So the dead children disappeared. Apart from the signs of fear and distress, there is no trace of them.

Something similar happens with child sexual abuse (abbreviated hereafter to csa). An abuse survivor once described it to me as 'soul-murder'; it is murder on a terrible scale, but most of the victims seem to disappear without trace. They are invisible as child-victims and later as adults; we are

1

rarely disturbed by them. Their lingering distress is occasionally signalled by apparently inexplicable bursts of grief or anger or depression.

In any church congregation of a hundred people there are probably at least ten who were subjected in childhood to sexual abuse which, in some cases, has had a disastrous effect on their physical and mental health. In any church school assembly, there are a number of pupils who are suffering or have suffered some kind of sexual abuse.

We must attend to abuse survivors and hear their story, if only for the sake of this other almost invisible group – children who are being sexually abused now, and who may carry the mental scars of abuse forever. Most of them cannot speak out; sexually abused children are silenced by threats and coercion, and the numbers who eventually contact a helpline or other source of help are a small proportion of the total. Therefore we must look to yesterday's victims to tell us something about what is happening to today's.

The Church's involvement

What is the relationship of the various Christian churches to this problem? Saturday 9 May 1992 saw the first church service in Britain held for survivors of csa. One of the organizers described some of the implications of being abused in a Christian family: 'One of our group members, a Catholic, was abused by her father, a regular churchgoer. There were crucifixes on the walls of her home, and when she goes to church now she gets flashbacks of being abused' (a 'flashback' is a sudden overwhelming sense of being back in, and re-experiencing, a traumatic situation from one's past).

Another survivor said: 'I prayed to God to stop the abuse and when he didn't, I felt he must be allowing it. This must be what I was put here for, to be abused.'

Csa is a problem at the heart of society, and therefore at the heart of the Church. It is not a problem 'out there' into which the Church may or may not decide to have an input. The Church is *already* involved in the following ways:

2

- abused children may come to the Church for help;
- abuse survivors may turn to the Church for help;
- some clergy were sexually abused as children, and need help and support from their colleagues, congregations and superiors;
- children may be abused by Christian family members;
- elements in religious upbringing, such as a sense of guilt and the duty of obedience, may be used to facilitate the abuse of children;
- the close association of religious belief and practice with csa (as in the story above of being abused in a room with a crucifix on the wall) presents particular problems for the Christian abuse survivor;
- some clergy molest children;
- Christ came to bring life and bring it more fully; csa brings death. It kills spiritually and physically. Many victims harm or kill themselves; many feel they are 'living dead'.

There is therefore *no option* but to be involved; the church is *inevitably* a source of either harm or healing. It cannot remain uninvolved, because it never was. This book will look at the different ways in which the Church may help, heal, hinder, collude or abuse.

Why children?

There is a danger, when the Church comes at last to address the problem of child sexual abuse, that it will see only the word 'sexual' and miss the crucial first and last words 'child abuse'.

Sex and sexual morality have always been problem areas for the church, and as such have naturally given rise to intense interest, debate, prohibition, legislation and satire. In 1992 the Roman Catholic Church in Ireland was rocked by the revelation that a bishop had been making payments to a former mistress and illegitimate child over many years. This fascination with sexual matters may result in attention being focused on the sexual element of csa, as if the abuse were almost a 'victimless sin' in the same way as, for example, a gay relationship, a priest's affair, or other transgressions of church law.

The risk is that csa, if included in the category of sexual transgressions currently under debate, will not be seen as the uniquely soul-destroying experience it undoubtedly is. One intelligent, socially aware Catholic priest with whom I raised the problem of csa responded by commenting on the need for more pastoral training on the problems of sexual development, child abuse, homosexuality and AIDS. This response disturbed me, because I do not believe discussion of abuse belongs in such a context. A good case can be made for liberalization of church attitudes on matters of adult consensual sexual behaviour. Csa is a different matter.

This is not an isolated case. A BBC Radio 4 programme called *Sins of the Flesh*, broadcast in May 1992, discussed Roman Catholic attitudes towards adultery, celibacy, gay relationships, AIDS and csa. Any useful discussion of abuse must first establish a proper context as its starting point, and remove the debate from the entirely separate arena of the rights and wrongs in the relationships of consenting adults.

The only relationship between the two questions is one of balance. A disproportionate amount of energy and attention pours into the debate about details of loving consensual adult relationships, while the question of unloving adult–child sexual exploitation is inadequately addressed. Links proposed between the two areas are commonly flawed or nonsensical. For instance, it used to be suggested, on the basis of no evidence whatsoever, that gay men are more likely than heterosexual men to abuse children. The churches, by condemning and marginalizing sexual minorities, may help to give credence to such dangerous red herrings.

Why sexual abuse?

I have suggested that the church should concentrate on the 'child abuse' element of the problem, rather than the sexual one, but here too there is an important caveat. Csa is in many ways an entirely different problem from other kinds of child abuse, for instance, physical abuse and neglect cannot be addressed in the same way. It is a deliberate and planned misuse of power over children. It commonly involves or coexists with emotional abuse, because it violates the child's deepest feelings and emotional development. However, the damage done by the use of children for adult sexual gratification seems a degree worse than the harm arising from stress, inadequacy or immaturity on the part of carers.

It is also less well understood than other kinds of abuse. Twenty years ago, childcare professionals were just beginning to understand and define the phenomenon of 'baby-battering'. Early work on it was greeted with the same kind of horror and disbelief that is now commonly expressed in the face of csa: 'How could anyone do that to a child, especially their own child? I can't believe it.' However, the evidence was there in the shape of bruises, broken bones and, sometimes, dead children, and society had to accept and learn about the facts of child-battering. As a result, a reasonably mature social response has been developed; there is some understanding of the problems that lead to child-beating, there is help on offer, and there is usually some hope of a good outcome.

Sexual abuse is different. It leaves few visible signs, and so remains secret and hidden. The battering parent may be desperate for help to stop hitting her child, and given the right counselling and support has a good chance of becoming a non-abusive parent. The sexually-abusing adult does not want to stop and will avoid attempts to investigate or stop the abuse. He will build a wall of threats, lies and silence to block out any interference. The pastoral care and support which may well help a battering family will have little effect in a family where a child is being sexually abused. The sexual abuser finds it almost impossible to stop, and is likely to use any pastoral input, as far as possible, to allow the abusive situation to continue undisturbed.

It is important, therefore, to have good information and a sound understanding of the aetiology of child sexual abuse, as a basis for addressing it. This book is not an attempt to supply all that information, which is well done elsewhere, but it does aim to establish a proper starting-point for the churches to look at the problem. This starting-point has three essential elements:

- commitment (it is already our problem);
- context (it should be classed neither with adult sexual transgression nor with child abuse in general);
- good information (rather than rumour, distortion, denial or minimization).

To achieve all three, we need to turn to the real experts – abuse survivors. They can tell us (those who have not locked the painful memories up beyond recall) what sexual abuse is like, what kind of damage it does, how it is carried out. They can help us to look at the peculiarly painful aspects of intrafamilial abuse – loving the abuser, while desperately wanting the abuse to stop; being forced to feel sexual sensations that may be pleasurable, but with someone they do not want to have such feelings with; turning the guilt and hatred in on themselves; feeling distant from and afraid to love their own children. This book acknowledges the authority of abuse survivors and honours their experience; this is the only valid starting point for an approach to csa. Respecting the expertise of survivors may, however, present difficulties in churches where the priest is seen as the pastoral expert, the authority on moral and sexual matters, and the mediator of healing.

To listen to survivors even for a short time is distressing; it is to glimpse the painful road they have to travel. As the woman at the Christian survivors' service said, 'The eternal question is why? Why me? Why did God let this happen? And there is no answer.'

Methodology and scope

This book is not comprehensive or large-scale. The writer is neither a childcare professional nor a theologian, but a Catholic mother with a background of community action to develop better child-protection.

The first-hand experiences recounted are mainly from two sources: a small survey among two London-based groups for Christian survivors of child sexual abuse, and personal contacts with groups and individuals in the northeast of England. There is no evidence to suggest that the incidence of abuse is any higher in this region than in any other, and I believe that anyone asking the same questions as I have asked in any other part of the country would find a similar picture.

When giving accounts of personal experiences of csa, I have changed the names of the people involved to protect their privacy.

Language

For the sake of brevity I have not constantly alluded to abusers and abuse victims as 'he or she'. Usually, but not always, I refer to the abuser as 'he', reflecting the fact that most but not all abusers are male (see chapter 2). Victims are both male and female, and I refer to them at different times as 'he' or 'she'.

The term 'abuse survivor' is used for any person who is trying to deal with the consequences of sexual abuse in his childhood. To some abused people it seems an ironic term; they feel that they are at best barely and precariously surviving. I have however chosen Poston and Lison's broad definition (used here in relation to women only):

> Manuals are written about steps to take in order to become a survivor rather than a victim . . . Checklists of what a woman must do to qualify as a survivor put a heavy burden upon women . . . We feel that any woman who is not in a cemetery is a survivor.[1]

I have used the terms 'Christianity' or 'the Church' to refer to the Christian Church or churches in general, unless a particular denomination is being discussed. I have tried not to make excessively general comments, and I hope that Christian readers will be able to discern which observations apply to their own church and which do not.

1

'I lost God'

Child sexual abuse – the words are familiar; what is the reality?
Chapter 2 sets out some facts and figures, but the right place
for this book to start is with the experience of abuse, its
meaning, what part it plays in the lives of its victims, how it
affects them and why.

Abuse within a Christian family

The story of Elizabeth, a young Tyneside nurse, gives a
glimpse of what it is like to grow up in the shadow of sexual
abuse, in the heart of a respectable churchgoing family.

■ I was abused by my father. I think it started when I was
about four, and went on till I left home – well, longer than that
really: till I got married. I left home at eighteen to do nursing
training, but I was still in London, so I still saw my father.

I was ill during my training, so it took me a long time to
qualify. I had anorexia. I suppose I did see links between my
illness and the abuse. It was still happening, and I was very
unhappy, and I just stopped eating. Nobody else knew the
reason though. They didn't ask the right questions and I didn't

tell them. I was sent to a psychiatrist who gave me a box of Complan and told me not to be a silly girl. Then the hospital sent me home – to my father – to recover! This was only about seven years ago. I stayed at home then till I got married.

After I married, my father no longer had sex with me but he used to do other things to me. When my first child was born he and my mother came to visit. When I saw him with my little girl in his arms, I just knew I was going to have to do something, to talk about what he'd done to me. I told my GP first, and he sent me for counselling by a psychiatric nurse. That didn't last long, I didn't find it very helpful. My GP hasn't got a clue really. He keeps asking how long I'm going to let it upset me – it's in the past, I should put it behind me.

I told my mother soon after their visit. She promptly had hysterics; didn't believe me, or said she didn't, and told my father. I've had no contact with him since. He wrote a letter and sent it to all the family, and other people – neighbours, GP, everybody – saying how wicked I was and how mentally disturbed I must be to make up such lies. The very last time I saw him, he wee'd all over the bathroom floor and then stood over me as I cleaned it up. He didn't touch me or anything, but I just did as he said. I'd done it for so long.

He used to make phone calls to me when I was at home on my own, very rude and obscene calls, and I never once hung up. I sat and listened to him.

My mother still believes and supports my father, so I don't see her either. We've had a few family meetings to discuss it, and she sometimes gets to the point of almost believing me, but then she goes home and goes back to believing him. My sister and sister-in-law are quite supportive to me though.

The first person I ever told was a priest, when I was about eleven or twelve. My father is a very religious man, he went to church every Sunday, and he used to take me along to confession each week. One week I told the priest about the abuse. It was a stupid thing to do because he knew my father well, and he just said that I must have got the wrong end of the stick, and he was sure that nothing bad at all had happened. He said that my father was a lovely man. I decided then that if that was what happened when you told people, I wouldn't tell anyone else.

10

Years later, at the church I went to when I first confronted my family, I told the priest there, and he said how difficult the situation must be, and he added: 'I feel so sorry for your father; think what all of this must be doing to him.' He had met my parents. He counselled me to forgive. I still see that priest from time to time; I feel ill when I see him.

But the deacon at my local church has been ever so helpful. I talked to her about the abuse, and she said she felt she didn't know enough about it, so she did a training course to understand it better.

She has been very involved in various family meetings, and has visited my parents. At one meeting my father said to her, 'Before God, I have never had sex with anyone but my wife.' She replied, 'Before God, you have.'

I worry about other children in the family. The only way they could be protected is if I made a statement to the police, and I'm just not ready to do that yet, not at the moment. But it's awful knowing that something may be happening to them and if I don't say anything it won't be stopped.

I find it difficult to talk about my abuse; I write about it a lot and get rid of it that way. I've been doing it ever since I was ill. I've been to an abuse survivors' group, but it wasn't for me. It was very hot and smoky in the room, and I was pregnant and feeling sick.

One of the worst times was when I was anorexic, because I had that to cope with as well as abuse. I've had ongoing problems with eating, things still aren't right now, but I've just gradually got better. As far as other people are concerned I was 'better' as soon as my weight was back up to a reasonable target, which I managed quite quickly. Everyone said, 'Haven't you got better quickly!'

Why didn't I say no to my father? It had gone on for such a long time, and I hated it, and he knew I hated it, but I still didn't try to stop it. It seemed better to get it over with. Even after I was married he used to visit me here.

He wasn't violent, at least not when I was older. When I was young he used to threaten me, and the things he did were a lot worse than later. Later on, I suppose I gave up protesting really. I was his daughter, I had to do as he said.

As I said, he was a regular churchgoer. Every time I go to

church I think: 'What on earth is this all about? Yes, I believe, but what has the Church got to do with my belief? Not a lot.'

Elizabeth's story, still unresolved, contains elements painfully familiar to other abuse survivors:

- Her compliance was enforced by violent and terrifying abuse, which became 'gentler' once she had learned that there was no possibility of escape.
- The abuser was a pillar of the community, scrupulous in his religious observance.
- When the child told a priest he replied that she was wrong. This seemed to her to bring the whole weight of the church's authority against her and in support of her abuser, and stifled any further attempts to seek help. One person who could have helped this child to achieve an abuse-free adolescence abandoned her to continuing abuse.
- She gave other signals of distress which should have evoked a helping response (anorexia, depression) but the health professionals around her failed to help her.
- Her abuser asserted his power over her, even after her disclosure, publicly by ridicule and privately by obscene phone calls and grotesquely disgusting behaviour in her house; he reviled and defiled her. He is still the powerful figure in the family, she the scapegoat for his actions.
- When she revealed the abuse in adulthood the priest's response was immediate sympathy for her father.
- She is still carrying, as well as her own distress, the weight of her family's problems resulting from the abuse (her mother's rejection, concern over possible risks to other children in the family).

In Elizabeth's case, the Church failed to help her in childhood. For some children, a religious background actually reinforces the guilt and terror of abuse. Rosemary, a Cleveland poet severely abused throughout childhood, describes a night in her childhood (like many abuse survivors she writes about herself in the third person with a pseudonym):

■ Sally was rudely awakened by heavy footsteps climbing the uncarpeted staircase. She felt the fear engulfing her body. What did he have on his mind tonight?

She heard a click as he put on the bedroom light, and the horrible sound of his heavy breathing. She tried to lie still and not shake with terror.

He quietly called her name and asked if she was awake. The little girl lay motionless but it didn't do any good. The sound of a zip being pulled and trousers hitting the floor. 'Mummy, why don't you stop him from hurting me? Why do you lie in bed pretending to be asleep?'

Suddenly all she can feel is agonizing pain, followed by a wet feeling that she knows is her own pee. She feels intensely sick and tears flow backwards into her ears. Her daddy tells her she is his little princess, and how much he loves her. All she can think of now is the trouble she will be in, in the morning when mummy finds out she has wet the bed again.

Now her bedroom is back in darkness, and she is left with the gremlins and goblins sent by the devil to haunt her. In Sunday School the previous week her uncle, the vicar, had told them what happened to naughty boys and girls. He told them the story about Adam and Eve being naked in the garden and how God was angry with them, and told them to put some clothes on. He said they were naughty not to wear clothes, and he would punish them for it. She remembered the story of Noah, and how all the boys and girls had been naughty and God had drowned them all. She had lain naked with her daddy, so God would punish her. What was he going to do to her? She cried herself to sleep.

The next morning, after she had been smacked for wetting the bed, she was packed off to school. In school, she sat thinking about all the horrible years her dad had been hurting her, and waiting for God to send down his punishment. She kept looking at the sky to make sure it wasn't going to rain.

In this case the child's normal Christian upbringing intensified the horror of her abuse. It is disturbing to find that Christianity, far from helping or comforting the abused child, can sometimes compound the abuse.

Church ministers who were abused in childhood

Adult survivors of csa who are also church ministers may face many troubling questions. Have they joined the ministry in a search for healing? Are they endeavouring to counsel and care for other victims of abuse without having fully resolved their feelings about their own abuse? Those who have faced up to and worked through their own trauma can be a source of wisdom and energy within the church.

I talked to an Anglican priest who was abused in his teens by his vicar:

■ It started when I was about fourteen I think. I was in the choir, and involved in things in the church. He began to invite a group of us up to the vicarage, all about the same age. We had a pleasant time in lots of ways. We'd drink cider, and play cards, and talk. Later in the evening when we were a bit drunk he would masturbate us.

I think he was troubled by what he did, but I think he couldn't stop himself. It stopped when I was about sixteen, because he died. I think it would have then anyway – that was his normal pattern, he started when a boy was about fourteen and after sixteen or so the abuse tailed off.

I remember one day I was at the vicarage and I was reading a leaflet about confession. It ended, 'The time to make your confession is now!' I was affected by it and when he came into the room I told him I wanted to make my confession. That threw him a bit, I think. He asked me (which he shouldn't really have done) what was on my conscience, what I wanted to confess. As far as I remember I was just getting into a sexual relationship with a girl – petting, and so on – and that was what it was about. As I was telling him he started to abuse me. I asked him not to, and he stopped.

I don't feel any great animosity towards him, I feel more pity than anger. I feel what he did was wrong, and I wish it hadn't happened, mainly because of the confusion it caused in me.

When my mother died I went to the chapel of rest where her body was lying, and it happened that this vicar was buried in

14

the same cemetery. I went to his grave and told him a few things, called him a few names.

Abuse survivors' problems with the patriarchal church

Margaret Kennedy[1] highlights the way in which sexual abuse in Christian families becomes entangled with the child's religious beliefs. She quotes abuse survivors:

■ I felt that the evil of abuse had made me evil and that there was no place for me in the church, only children who were good and pure were loved by God.

■ I'd say to myself, if I'm good from now on God will stop him doing these things to me. So whenever he'd come into my bedroom I knew I must have been bad.

Sometimes the links between abuse and religion are reinforced, if the child is abused or reabused by a priest: 'It took me three months to tell the priest about the abuse. He was affectionate and concerned – then later he abused me too.'
Kennedy comments:

> Many find it difficult to trust a male God or a male priesthood. God–human father–priest have become one. These are the powerful ones, they are the powerless. In my group of women four out of nine members were also molested by priests/ministers as children and two as adults.

This raises the difficult question of power and patriarchy. Most churches are hierarchical in structure, some extremely so. Most hierarchies are male-dominated; some exclude women almost entirely. Such a patriarchal structure has a particular resonance for the abused child or abuse survivor, especially where the abuser was her father. Language referring to God as father may identify God as an abuser. Feelings of guilt for allowing the abuse are paralleled by feelings of impurity and worthlessness in spiritual terms. The victim feels helpless at the hands of man and of God, crushed by adult and divine authority. (Abuse by women religious is also, of course, very damaging, but is not associated with hierarchical power in the same way as abuse by men. This is not to say that women do not sometimes abuse power when they hold it.)

Examining the experience of survivors, then, presents an immediate challenge to the churches. In their hierarchical structure and language of power they too often parallel the victim's experience of abuse. Whatever its good intentions, the church may look and feel to the abuse victim like an abusive structure.

Abuse by church ministers

During the months when I was preparing this book, I was surprised to hear more and more accounts of abuse within a Christian context, even by clergy or Christian community leaders. Such accounts were not confined to weird sects: they related to the whole range of Christian denominations. A common factor was the heightened sense of guilt, confusion and fear of punishment that arose from doing something perceived as sinful with and at the behest of someone perceived as holy.

This was the case with Dee, who narrates her story in the book *Home Is Where the Hurt Is*:[2]

■ I'm in the study again with grandfather. He is wearing his usual black suit and white dog collar. Now he puts his hand inside my knickers. The other hand is fiddling with his trouser zip. I don't know what he's doing. I can see something pink that he wants me to hold. He has a funny look in his eyes. 'We must keep it a secret', he says, doing up his zip when mother calls for me. I don't understand secrets.

. . . Grandfather is taking me to the church cellar to play a game. He opens the door with a rusty old key. With a creak, it opens. I don't like it inside. It smells damp and it's cold and dark. He shuts the door behind us. Grandfather takes my hand and leads me down the concrete steps. I feel unsure, even though he holds my hand.

I look around. Beside the steps is a great big pile of coal. Grandfather says it's for heating the church, then he shows me the boiler. He opens the door, the heat that comes out is great and it's all fiery inside.

He leaves the boiler door open, his face looks all red by the heat of the fire and I can see the firelight reflected in his glasses. It makes his eyes look red and wild. Then he holds me by the waist and kisses me on the mouth . . .

Then he stands up and leans against the bell. I can't really see what he's doing but he calls me over. He makes me hold something warm, which comes out of his trousers. I can't see what it is, but it feels the same as the pink thing did in the study. I don't understand it. He tells me to rub it and it goes hard.

I can still see his eyes though, they look all red and frightening. I'm starting to cry. Then I can't, something is in my mouth stopping me, I can hardly breathe. Choking, suffocating, terror.

I can't get away. He's holding me down. Grandfather says I must do it or I'll go into the fire. Something warm and sticky shoots into my mouth and trickles down my throat. Then it's all over, the thing is taken away. I want to be sick, the taste is so awful and my mouth hurts. I want to cry, but he tells me I mustn't.

I don't like these sort of games.

I'm outside now in the bushes, beside the church. Sitting down, holding my knees and crying softly, in case he hears me. I feel confused, dirty and horrid. I want to go to my mother, but I am frightened she'll tell me I'm a naughty girl for being dirty. I must be a good girl, I don't want to go into that fiery hell again.

Dee's abuse was reinforced by the power and authority of her abuser, as head of the family and Christian minister, God's representative, gatekeeper of heaven and hell. Four-year-old Dee actually sees hell gaping for her if she disobeys him – yet she knows what he does to her is wrong.

The terminology of survivors and surviving can give the impression that there is usually some kind of happy ending. It is important to remember that many do not survive, and to understand why. An experience like Dee's may not be surviv-able. In later life she found no happy ending. She suffered depression, compounded by well-meaning professionals who had no insight into her distress. She lost her children; she mutilated and tried to kill herself many times; she spent months in psychiatric hospitals.

> The last time I visited Dee in her home she had totally given up. She sat mutilated, alone, afraid. Her bath was full of burn holes, and her face and arms were slashed with cuts from glass. She had lost her reason to live.[3]

Abuse by clergy is a problem that most churches have been slow to acknowledge. On the few occasions when it is revealed it is treated as individual aberration, the 'one bad apple', and hushed up as far as possible. This is disastrous not only for the victims whose pain is minimized, but for the other children who will fall victim to the abusive minister.

A series of horrifying cases has focused attention recently on the Roman Catholic Church, though there is no reason to believe that csa is more or less prevalent in that church than in others. A particularly shocking scandal broke in Newfound-land, Canada, in 1988–89:

> Sixteen priests, former priests and members of the Christian Brothers, a celibate order that operates an orphanage in the city of St John's, have been charged with sex offences on the island. Two priests, both in their mid-fifties, have been convicted of a total of 27 charges of molesting altar boys over the past 18 years in their remote village parishes. The boys were given alcohol and drugs and forced to perform sex acts with the priests and with each other.[4]

The Church's subsequent report on the affair noted that the Archbishop of Newfoundland and his staff had been receiving reports of child molestation by priests and religious since 1975, but had taken no action.

In 1988 Fr Anton Mowat, a British priest who had been moved to America following allegations of child-molesting, fled from Georgia to Turin in Italy after renewed allegations of abuse. The Catholic hierarchy shielded him for two years while the American police launched an international manhunt for him. When he was finally arrested, in Darlington, England, he was training to be a paediatric nurse.[5]

In July 1992 seven former choirboys sued Fr James Porter, a former parish priest from Bemidji, Minnesota, who admitted abusing them: 'I was a sick man when I was a Roman Catholic priest in the 1960s. As a result of my illness, I sexually assaulted a number of children.'[6]

In December 1988 an enormous hoard of child pornography was discovered in the home of Roman Catholic priest Dino Cinel, in New Orleans. It included:

> 160 hours of home-made pornographic videotapes in which the handsome priest performed anal sex, oral sex, group sex and a dizzying array of other diversions (often including his fluffy white lapdog) with at least seven different teenage boys . . . To the horror of the parishioners at St Rita's, many of the videotapes were made in the rectory, in Fr Cinel's modest little suite of rooms right under the noses of the other priests in residence there.

Two young men later sued Fr Cinel. Now in their twenties, both are still deeply disturbed by the abuse. One of them 'remains particularly fragile; he has been diagnosed in the past as both suicidal and, after threatening to kill Cinel, homicidal, and he is haunted by his feelings of betrayal by the priest.'[7]

Cinel says he himself was sexually abused by his headmaster in Italy, an eminent priest and friend of the Pope.[8] This may or may not be true; it is a common legal defence in abuse cases for the abuser to assert that he was abused in childhood. (This is one of the factors contributing to the myth that abused children go on to become abusers.)

In mid-1992 it was revealed that four priests were receiving treatment at a Birmingham clinic for sex offenders. Ray Wyre, the director, said he had been 'overwhelmed' by the number of clergy abuse cases in the preceding year, and welcomed the Church's growing openness and willingness to seek treatment for abusers.[9]

In the USA, litigation rather than conscience may bring about more open and honest discussion of the problem. Since 1985, over $300 million has been paid by church officials and insurers to youngsters abused by clergy, and for associated medical and legal fees; it may be that a financial crisis will force the problem into the open.

Abuse by clergy seems to get subsumed into and camouflaged among the sex-scandal industry, where all clerical sexual transgressions are greeted with salacious glee by the gutter press and announced in glaring headlines. In 1992, the Eamonn Casey affair – the discovery of an Irish bishop's teenage son and former mistress – generated much debate, both serious and frivolous. An abuse survivor commented to me, 'What does it matter if priests have affairs and children? It's the ones who abuse we should be worrying about.' She told me about a friend who was deeply and chronically depressed following years of sexual abuse by a priest in Ireland.

■ It started when she was only two. He would carry her on his shoulders, and she would have a knee-length dress on. He was everybody's favourite 'uncle', jolly and popular. He would be holding her on his shoulders, not two yards from her parents, holding her by her thighs and actually penetrating her with his finger. She remembers that it hurt, and she felt really confused, because there were mum and dad and they weren't saying anything, and they must know, surely? And he was the priest, the voice of God, very powerful to such a little girl.

Child-molesting by Roman Catholic clergy is often discussed with reference to celibacy; they may be thought to be particularly prone to such temptations because of this vow. This is a mistake, since csa has more to do with misuse of power than with sexuality. Many active paedophiles have one or more sexual relationships with adults. Abuse by clergy does not arise from unbearable sexual frustration. Whether paedophiles are drawn to the priesthood because of the associated power and access to children remains an open question.

Sexual exploitation of the abuse survivor

Sexual abuse in childhood gives rise to feelings of powerless-ness, worthlessness and contamination which persist into adulthood. The abused person may feel she has nothing to offer but sex, that no one could love her for herself, that she has no rights over her own body. The vulnerability of abuse survivors presents a challenge to those caring for them; clergy in particular have a duty not to abuse the pastoral relationship nor betray their trust. Such a betrayal is devastating to the abuse survivor, who experiences it as reabuse. This is what happened to Susan, a young woman who lives in County Durham:

■ I was abused by a neighbour. It first happened when I was three. I was somewhere I shouldn't have been at the time, so I felt it was my fault. I couldn't tell anyone, or I would have got a good hiding for being naughty.

When I was seven, I started going to confession. Every time, I would tell the priest what was happening, because I thought it was a sin, you see – my sin – but he just ignored it, gave me the usual three Hail Marys or whatever, without comment.

The abuse culminated in full intercourse when I was thir-teen, and I told my mother. All hell was let loose. The man wasn't prosecuted, but my brothers beat him up. My mother wasn't very helpful, she was mainly worried about what the neighbours would think. I felt terrible, I felt like everybody blamed me. The only person who really seemed to care about me was this young priest, Father Greg. He listened to me, and said the right things. He was great with me. When I felt everyone was blaming me, I went off the rails, I was quite promiscuous; and he would go crazy with me: 'What are you doing? You've got to stop doing this!' He was there to help me get through – he was the only one that accepted me and cared about me. I could talk to him about anything, I really loved him. We stayed great friends for years.

When I was going to get married he seemed really against it and warned me off, which I thought was a bit odd. But he bought us a wedding present. Then he was sent back to Ireland for two years, and I didn't see him during that time.

After I was married, and he had come back from Ireland, he came to visit us. We hadn't seen each other for ages, and we sat up talking till late at night, after my husband had gone to bed. When we got up to go to bed, it was late as we'd been talking and talking, and he said, 'Can I have a goodnight kiss?' I thought, 'What's he on about?' He'd never even hugged me, never mind wanted to kiss me, all the time I'd known him. So I went over to give him a quick kiss on the cheek, and that's not the way he kissed me at all, and it terrified me and I pulled away, and he just kept a hold of me. I thought, 'Oh, God, what's happening?' I wasn't frightened of him, it was the fact that he was a priest, that was all that was in my mind: 'They don't do this, this doesn't happen with priests.'

Next morning, Greg said he was sorry about what had happened the night before. I said to myself, 'Calm down, it's all right, don't worry about it.' I suggested a walk, and I showed him the village, but when we got to the riverside, he grabbed me again. But now, it was like he was assuming it must be all right! He had his gear on, dog collar and all, anyone could have seen him, and he just didn't care. He wasn't embarrassed or worried at all – I was, but he wasn't.

It seemed to be, that I'd taken my problems to him when I was younger, and he'd helped me, and I really needed him, and I was grateful – but now it was payback time. I hadn't understood there would be a price to pay, but there was. I did love him for his kindness, and I needed to talk to him, but I didn't want sex with him. But he made me feel I owed it to him.

Before all this, I'd always felt very safe with priests. Not any more. There was no one left to turn to. When I wanted to go to confession, Greg would have been the first priest I'd turn to, but of course I couldn't. My parish priest would be the next, and when I went to him for confession, and told him about all this, he said I was prostituting myself to this priest and I must stop. He didn't say anything about it being his colleague, though he must have known. He didn't suggest how I could stop it, or that Greg ought to stop.

When I walked out of the confessional I felt I was going crazy. I thought 'Is nobody going to help me? How can I stop this?' Greg had told me that if I was to say anything, nobody would believe me. They'd believe him, because he was a priest. But when I tried to stop him, saying he shouldn't touch me because he was a priest, he said he wasn't a priest first and foremost, he was a man. It did my head in.

I felt that terrible and guilty, I can't tell you. Sometimes I feel like shaking him and yelling, 'Do you know what you did to me?'

Susan's feelings are familiar to abuse victims – self-blame, feelings of obligation towards the abuser, rage, despair. She wants him at least to realize how much he has hurt her, but she knows he will deny it to others, to her and to himself. Her hurt is invisible to him.

Betrayal by the one person who had befriended her compounded the childhood abuse. Abuse of any pastoral relationship is damaging; in the case of a priest who is seen in some senses as God's representative on earth, the shock and confusion are worse. Colin Carr, a Dominican prior who has counselled several abuse survivors, emphasizes the positive contribution of celibacy to the pastoral relationship: 'The point about celibacy is that it should make you a safe person for the people who need you. Someone who has been hurt should be able to come to you knowing that you are not going to abuse their trust.' Father Greg's reabuse of Susan drove her out of her church:

■ Later I met someone from the church I go to now, the Church of Christ, and I started going to that. After a while I told the ministers about what was happening, and they were wonderful. They sorted me out with a Christian therapist, and they helped me to see that I hadn't condemned myself to hell, and that God still cared about me. Before that, Greg had represented God to me, in a way, caring for me after other people in my life had abused me, so when he abused me, it messed me up completely. It wiped out all the good things. I lost God, and I lost the Church, when he did that to me – and the Catholic Church had meant a great deal to me. Priests are supposed to bring you closer to God, and help your faith – he stripped me of my faith.

He's probably doing the same thing to some other vulnerable young woman. If I knew he was I would go straight to the bishop and tell him. But he wouldn't believe me, would he? He wouldn't believe me over Greg. Greg's quite high up now, he's got his own parish.

In the women's refuge where she now works, Susan has encountered victims of Christian abusers. One young woman in particular stays in her mind:

■ She had been in care from an early age, in a convent school. One of the helpers, a young man, used to abuse her. She was only four, and one night he used scissors on her, and a baseball bat. Next morning the nuns saw blood on her bed, and they called her a wicked girl, and cut off her long fair hair.

She was so badly abused, that bairn, I don't know if she'll ever recover. She's twenty-five now, and she's a drug addict. She thinks she's an evil person. The abuser went on to train for the priesthood.

When I heard her story, I could have gone and smashed all the Catholic church windows. I was fuming. These are people you are supposed to go to if you need help, and look what they did to her.

When I heard what had happened to her, it made me cry, and I'm not a crier. I thought of what had been done to her and what had been done to me and I thought, well, where is God? He wasn't there for us, that's for sure.

Religion based on fear

Though there is no reason to believe abuse is more common in some sects or denominations than in others, it may be that in the more fierce and punitive sects there is a greater degree of terror involved. This was the experience of Dorothy, a Tyneside teacher:

■ I was brought up as a member of the Exclusive Brethren. I was sexually abused by my father, who was Brethren, the lodger, who was Methodist, and a neighbour, who was Roman Catholic. That's my own personal black joke, that I was ecumenically abused. I was also emotionally abused and neglected. I think I was also sexually abused by my brother, who's thirteen years older than me. I believe he was abused, and I know he went on to become an abuser. Later on my father abused my young niece.

A lot of the men who abused me had a religious dimension to their lives, and in the last couple of years I've been thinking about that and realizing that there is probably a lot of it going on in the churches. I'd like to help with initiatives to try to deal with that.

My father was a Leader of the Brethren. My theory is that abusers crave respectability, and through the church they can get that respectability, as well as other things – access to children, a cloak of piety, good feelings about themselves, absolution. I dread to think how many other children he abused.

In the Exclusive Brethren the men are given a lot of power and authority. The women and children have to be silent and obedient. I think that situation is abusive in itself. That amount of arbitrary power is bound to be misused.

Here once again is the abuse survivor's challenge to male-dominated, hierarchical churches. If such power carries the probability or certainty that it will be used to abuse and terrorize children, how can we justify imposing that authority and power over children? It suggests that the churches should look at themselves very critically to see whether they are safe for children.

Churches have traditionally opted out of the framework of human rights and civil liberties demanded by secular culture (the Church of England, for instance, insisted on being excluded from the Equal Opportunities Act). The implication is that they will act justly without secular regulation. Much of women's and children's experience challenges this.

Dorothy recognizes that an authoritarian church may be simply a convenient framework for parents who would be cold and rejecting in any circumstances, but she vividly conveys the added terror of the supernatural dimension of her abuse:

■ The Brethren . . . have this idea of the Rapture, that

Christ will literally come to earth at any moment and carry off all those who are saved and leave the damned behind to face the end of the world – famine, pestilence, and so on. It was terrifying imagery, and I used to hear all this constantly as a child. When I was about six I started to have nightmares about it. By then I was already being abused, and had all the guilt feelings about that, and I was sure I was damned. I remember having a nightmare and getting into my mum's bed and saying to her, 'If Jesus comes back and I'm not saved, will he take you and leave me behind?' She said 'Yes.' I said, 'What if I find a chain and chain myself to you, won't I get taken as well?' 'No, you'd be left behind', she said. After that, I went round the house and looked in all the cupboards to find out where the food was, and I learned to use a tin-opener, because I thought, 'When they go, I'll have to take care of myself.' If I came in and there was no one in I would panic, because I thought they'd already gone. (That's still with me, I still get that feeling of panic.) One night I woke up and there was no one in the house, and I ran in my bare feet through the backyard to my grandparents' house, thinking, please, please let them be there, if my grandparents are still there then it hasn't happened. It was sheer terror.

The religious input, on top of the sexual abuse, was very damaging.

Dorothy also mentions the role of the church as a framework for inter-generational abuse:

■ I think the abuse and the religion had been hand in hand for a long time. I found out later that my mother's mother had had some sort of massive breakdown and believed that she was damned. She kept saying, 'I'm a wicked, wicked woman.' She was also anorexic, which is a common result of abuse.

An outsider might expect a church community to be particularly shocked and condemnatory when abuse is revealed, but Dorothy's story shows a sadly more typical outcome – concealment and containment.

■ I've blocked out a lot of memories of when I was four and

five. All I have left is glimpses – of an erect penis, and that when they read from the Bible about 'Abraham and his seed', I knew what seed looked like. I remember coming out of my dad's workshop, and the whole world spinning round me in a turmoil. The later abuse, the neighbour and the man who stayed with us, I do remember that in detail.

Then later, all of a sudden, my dad stopped speaking to me. At first I was his princess and his treasure and his bag of gold, then suddenly it stopped. He never spoke to me for the rest of his life. I've had to turn detective to work out what was going on, but I think the time he stopped was when it had been found out that he had abused two other girls in the Brethren meeting. I suspect he was threatened or pressured in some way, and at that time he cut off from me, though he may have found other victims elsewhere. My father took the line that these girls had led him on, it was their idea. All the Brethren did was exclude him from fellowship for a while. They didn't do anything to protect other children from him. Obviously they didn't involve any other agency, because Brethren have to keep separate. I think all these sects which are very self-contained and insist on being separate from the rest of the world are ideal for abusers, because they won't be reported. It's the perfect self-contained unit, its own little world, and any intervention from secular agencies is seen as persecution. Anyone who appeals to an outside agency may be harassed and cast out from the community. And of course if that little community is your whole world, to be cast out of it is devastating.

This is a common feature of many sects and religions, not just Christian churches. In 1991 there was a campaign of harassment and intimidation against an orthodox Jewish family whose child had been sexually abused by a member of their community:

> A Jewish family from Stamford Hill, north London, whose six-year-old daughter was sexually abused by a teenager from their religious community, are now at a secret address after their home was besieged by a mob. The family went into hiding after a crowd of orthodox

Jews marched at midnight to their house and threw bricks while shouting 'Informers.' . . . Police revealed last night that the family had suffered an 18-month ordeal of hostility. Police said that between 100 and 200 protesters threw missiles at the family's home . . . the family had moved home five times in the past year under the pressure of hostility.[10]

The charges in this case were labelled anti-Semitism. Concerns of abuse of children and women in Muslim families may be labelled racist, according to Pragna Patel of Southall Black Sisters: 'We are constantly told that to raise our voices in public is to invite a racist backlash, yet we have to confront daily violence, abuse, rape and harassment of women.'[11]

Every sect and religion is very defensive about abuse: 'It's not a problem for us, it doesn't happen among Jews/Brethren/Hindus/Muslims/Catholics . . .' As a result there are few or no steps taken to protect children in the community from known abusers. It would be a giant step forward if each community would accept that sexual abuse exists in all social and religious groups, and seek ways of dealing with it.

2

Facts and figures

There is a nervous feeling around that the factual background of child sexual abuse is murky and polemical, to be understood only by a few professionals. Actually a lot of it is very straightforward; the basic facts could and should be a matter of common knowledge. This chapter will attempt not a review of all that is known about it, but a summary of some of the basic information and ways of coming to understand it better. Any Christian attempt to help, however well intentioned, will be inadequate if it is not grounded in an understanding of child sexual abuse – how common it is, the dynamics of power and manipulation, the ways in which abusers target and groom children; the difficulty of stopping paedophilic behaviour; the types of help needed by abused childen and their carers.

What is child sexual abuse?

Many definitions have been framed, some very long as they try to include all the various manifestations of child sexual abuse. Baker and Duncan[1] suggest the following:

> A child (anyone under sixteen years) is sexually abused

29

when another person, who is sexually mature, involves the child in any activity which the other person expects to lead to their sexual arousal.

Schecter and Roberge's definition[2] is also widely used:

Sexual abuse is defined as the involvement of dependent, developmentally immature children and adolescents in sexual activities they do not truly comprehend, to which they are unable to give informed consent, or that violate the social taboos of family roles.

The first definition includes the important element of sexual gratification. Adults sometimes react defensively when csa is discussed, complaining, 'I don't know any more what I can safely do with my children. What about bathing my baby? What about my daughter sitting in my lap? Is that abusive or not?' The straightforward answer is, 'Do you become sexually aroused doing it?' Adults know well enough when they are doing something for their own sexual gratification. Children must not be used for adult sexual satisfaction – not because children are not sexual beings, but because their bodies and their sexuality belong to themselves and to no one else, and are particularly precious for being so vulnerable. Moreover, sexual development is gradual and depends on a constellation of factors: awareness of self and others, choice, relationship, equality and mutuality, exploration and discovery, autonomy. This process is disastrously disrupted if adult sexual acts intrude on a young person's sexual development.

The second definition adds another important element, that of consent. Abusers frequently assert or hint that their victims consented to sex with them. Glaser and Frosh[3] point out that this is always a falsehood, whatever the circumstances, because of the inequality of power between adults and children:

Children are *structurally* dependent on adults; that is, their dependence is one of the factors that defines them as children. Sexual activity between an adult and a child thus always designates an exploitation of power; in this respect, it differs from other forms of sexual encounter and can never be anything but abuse.

Prevalence

The research evidence about prevalence falls into two catego-
ries: numbers of children currently known to be suffering csa
or where csa is strongly suspected, and surveys of adults,
assessing the numbers who recollect abuse in childhood. The
latter category is generally accepted as more accurate; all
child-protection agencies agree that the number of children
who reveal abuse while it is happening is a fraction of the
number of actual victims.[4]

The surveys of adults throw up results that are varied but
complementary rather than conflicting. For example, Finkelhor, one of the most respected authorities on the subject,
carried out a national survey in the USA in 1990 which
produced figures of 27 per cent (women) and 16 per cent (men)
who had suffered some form of sexual abuse in childhood.[5] A
British study by Nash and West[6] suggested an incidence figure
of 46 per cent for women. Nash and West used a wider
definition of sexual abuse than Finkelhor. A wider definition,
however, does not necessarily trawl a greater number of 'less
severe incidents'. Researchers have to choose some definition,
but most now are careful not to impose a scale of seriousness.
For example, a violent rape of a child by a stranger may be less
traumatic in the long run, if the parents believe and protect the
child, than habitual 'gentle' or non-contact abuse (e.g. use of
pornography by a parent to degrade a child, or regular
'flashing' at a child), with the resultant feelings of confusion
and betrayal.

An often-quoted figure is the MORI poll of 1985,[7] which
gave an incidence of 10 per cent (8 cent of men, 12 per cent of
women). This is a useful, well-established statistic to
remember, while bearing in mind that wider definitions of
sexual abuse or more in-depth studies have yielded higher
figures. Where the opportunity to remember and speak out is
present, much higher figures commonly emerge. Sandra, a
Yorkshire minister's wife, counsels abuse survivors among
her church members:

> Because they know I am a survivor, and will understand
> and know what they are talking about, lots of survivors

turn to me for help who otherwise wouldn't say anything to anybody. So I come across a lot of abuse – much higher than the quoted statistics.

It used to be thought that girls are three times as likely as boys to be sexually abused. The extent of under-reporting makes it impossible to be sure, but it is currently thought that the ratio is more like three to two.[8] There is some evidence that among the under-sevens the ratio is more even.[9] There may be both physical and social reasons for this. Little children of both sexes are easy to overpower, whereas among older children boys are likely to be more assertive than girls. In little children, penetrative abuse is often anal, and for anal abuse either sex will serve as victim. After puberty girls are more likely to be victimized than boys; or to put it another way, sexual abuse of boys is more likely to diminish or stop at this age, while abuse of girls is more likely to be initiated or continue.

Damage

The harm done by sexual abuse has been obscured by myths and misconceptions, many of them identical with the justifications given by abusers for their behaviour: 'It doesn't do any real harm', 'He'll soon get over it', 'She seems perfectly OK'. This ignorance is found at all levels, right up to the judiciary. Sentencing policy in English courts has sometimes mirrored the abuser's tendency to put the blame on his victim, his wife, anyone but himself. For example, a 62-year-old man who had had sex with a 13-year-old girl was given a light sentence because, said the judge, the girl was 'depraved'.[10]

The harm done by abuse is almost limitless, and extends across the range of physical, mental and spiritual health. In little children, signs and symptoms can include genital and anal trauma, regression, sexualized behaviour, sexually transmitted diseases, failure to thrive (a striking symptom – in the face of such unloving behaviour, the infant simply stops growing and pines, however well fed and otherwise cared for). Little children may also show precocious sexual knowledge and behaviour: a foster mother described her three-year-old foster child's behaviour in this way:

■ She bit herself and picked wounds in herself until blood ran, and poked her fingers into her eyes as blind children often do . . . She masturbated to the exclusion of any other activity and rubbed herself against any male she came in contact with . . . Her behaviour to men was openly and sexually provocative, and it was confusing to see such a small child exhibiting all the awareness of a sexually active teenager . . . Where other children gave simple affection she had learned to respond in an openly sexual manner.[11]

School-age children may show depression and low self-esteem, problems at school, psychosomatic reactions, anal and genital symptoms such as itching and bleeding, and sexually transmitted disease including AIDS. (AIDS is a new dimension of the harm done to sexually abused children. It is comparatively rare in Britain as yet, but a 1992 BBC radio news report found that nineteen out of twenty child prostitutes in a brothel in Thailand were HIV positive.) Emotional signs include anger, despair, shame, guilt and distrust of adults. Conversely they may present as extremely good children, desperate not to draw attention to themselves and incur adult censure.

Adolescents may display various kinds of disturbed behaviour: depression, school avoidance, running away, self-mutilation, eating disorders, sexually transmitted disease including AIDS, pregnancy.

In adulthood symptoms include severe mood-swings, suicide attempts, multiple personality disorder, sexual dysfunction, relationship breakdown, mental illness, sterility, pelvic disease, AIDS. It is often forgotten that childhood sexual abuse can damage physical health just as badly as mental health. A recent study in the *British Medical Journal*[12] looked at a group of psychiatric patients who had suffered sexual abuse in childhood and had undergone extensive surgery in adulthood. Their surgical involvement had included the following specialities: breast surgery, cardiology, dermatology, ear, nose and throat, endocrinology, gastroenterology, haematology, neurology, obstetrics, orthopaedics, rheumatology, urology, pain clinic. Had their doctors discovered and understood the connection between their childhood abuse and their adult illness, they might have been spared excessive surgery, and a more effective route to healing might have been sought.

Why do some abused children suffer worse consequences than others? The damage is partly correlated with the severity and duration of the abuse, and whether or not the child has found a believing and supportive adult to help him. But that is not a complete explanation. We have no way of predicting which children will make a quick and good recovery and which have been hurt so deeply they may never recover completely. For that reason there should be a presumption in every case that the abused child needs the abuse to be stopped and therapy to be provided; '[to] the question of when intervention is necessary . . . the general answer can only be "always".'[13] The child has an absolute right and need to have the abuse stopped. This should not be compromised by assertions that intervention will be too traumatic for the child and family. We should be pursuing the goal of first-class intervention, therapy, support for carers, interim childcare if needed, rather than using any shortcomings in such provision as an excuse to sanction continuing abuse of a child.

In popular reporting of abuse, the discovery of the abuse, and subsequent court case or other sequel, is seen as an ending, a resolution. In fact for the few victims whose abuse is revealed it is only a beginning; if they are lucky enough to receive appropriate help, it is the beginning of a shaky and uncertain path towards healing. For others it is simply a slight interruption in a 'career' of abuse which will continue when the abuser leaves prison and rejoins the family, or when another abuser targets the vulnerable child.

Who are the abusers?

Most abusers are known to their victims; they are family members or friends. Most victims are abused by 'safe' people in 'safe' places. This makes it harder for them to be believed and get help and protection. A Childwatch survey found that six out of ten children had tried to speak out about their abuse but it had made no difference (or had actually made things worse).[14]

Most male abusers are not measurably different psychologically from other males. They are normal members of the population:

> The uncomfortable fact is that abusers do *not* stand out from 'the rest of us'; they are your neighbours, your friends, your colleagues, your doctor, your solicitor, your social worker, your family – maybe even yourself. They come from all walks of life and all classes: judges and directors of social services have been found guilty of sexual assault upon children.[15]

Most abusers (over 90 per cent) are male,[16] except in cases of ritual abuse where the picture is different (see chapter 7). It is important to remember that some children are sexually abused by women; denial of the existence of female perpetrators is oppressive to abuse survivors who were victimized by women. Csa by women is currently being taken more seriously, notably by Elliott.[17] The problem as a whole, however, should be addressed as one of male abuse of power.

Some men take offence at this approach, as if it were a personal attack rather than a social analysis. Yet any injustice which shows a pattern of being perpetrated by one group against another – such as apartheid in South Africa – requires an analysis of the system which allows or encourages such injustice. An analogy closer to home is the problem of domestic violence, which is accepted to be mainly a crime of men against women. Men are on average more powerful physically, financially and socially than women, and any such power imbalance tends to lead to abuse.

This is not a criticism of individual men, it is an observation of a gender problem; not a weapon in a feminist war on men, but a social analysis which could be a tool for social healing. The few cases where women are the abusers do not invalidate this analysis (though they should not be overlooked) just as the few cases where women beat up men do not change the fact that domestic violence is a problem of the social construction of maleness. The triumphant declaration, 'Women do it too, you know!' too often masks a refusal to address the problem at all.

It is a pity that some well-intentioned men are so defensive about this fact, because defensiveness stands in the way of understanding and child-protection. Borrowdale encountered this reaction in men she spoke to on the subject: 'It is interesting, though sad, that the major way in which men reacted was not with horror that fathers could abuse children, but with feeling threatened that *they* might be suspected.'[18] In other words, women think, 'What if that happened to my child?' while men think, 'What if that accusation were directed at me?'

Borrowdale makes the point that the gender difference does not mean that women are more virtuous than men by nature. Women hurt children in various ways, but not (on the whole) by sexual abuse.

It is often forgotten that it is the women's movement which is largely responsible for revealing the problem of csa and initiating research on it. Many Christians place feminism so firmly in their demonology that they have a kneejerk adverse reaction to anything coming from a feminist source, and this may account for some of the inadequacies in the churches' approach to the problem. Keith Pringle, a social science lecturer who has researched the sensitive problem of safe foster placements for abused youngsters, insists that the feminist model provides the best analysis of why abuse happens, though he favours an eclectic approach which draws on other models as well:

> The statistics . . . and our own practice strongly indicate that in the vast majority of cases of sexual abuse one model has a far greater potential for explanation than any of the others: the feminist model. Increasingly other mainstream commentators are coming to the conclusion that male socialisation is a major factor in sexual abuse . . . We would agree with Glaser/Frosh, Mary McLeod/ Esther Saraga and Liz Kelly that male socialisation and patriarchy is *the* major factor in sexual abuse. We do, of course, recognise that other models have some value, to a greater or a lesser extent, depending on the case: the power model, certainly; the cycle of abuse theory, sometimes; we might even consider some aspects of the family model in a few situations.[19]

36

In Christian terms, this might indicate, as Margaret Kennedy suggested in a sermon in Cambridge in October 1992, that patriarchy is in itself abusive and sinful.

Do victims become abusers?

One myth that is paraded over and over again – almost the only 'fact' that some people seem to know about child sexual abuse – is that abused children commonly turn into abusers. This unproved assertion is based on the 'cycle of abuse' theory which, according to researcher Liz Kelly,

> has proved a popular explanation for all forms of physical and sexual abuse within the family, explaining complex social phenomena using simplistic behavioural and individualistic models . . . 'Cycle of abuse' models embody a determinism which is damaging to practice: experience A leads to behaviour B with minimal choice/agency in between. These models, apart from offering abusers the excuse to avoid responsibility, also make the thousands of survivors who, as a result of their own experiences, choose never to treat children in similar ways, invisible or logically impossible.[20]

Kelly points out that if the cycle of abuse theory were accurate, women abusers would outnumber men by about three to two, rather than male abusers outnumbering female by more than nine to one.

Evidence cited in favour of the cycle of abuse theory tends to be anecdotal or based on flawed research, including a study carried out among prisoners in the USA. Prison populations are not typical of the population as a whole, and in any case since we do not know accurately the level of csa in the general population it is impossible to judge whether a particular group of convicted sex offenders shows a higher rate of childhood sexual trauma than the population average.

The implication that victims become abusers is offensive and destructive to victims struggling to survive and rebuild their lives. It undermines their own parenting skills and their fragile self-esteem.

What is true, however, is that abuse makes children vulnerable in all sorts of ways: to renewed victimization, and in some cases to the impulse to treat other children the way they were treated. Most survivors, especially women, resist this impulse: yet their vulnerability must be taken seriously, and appropriate therapy and support given to strengthen the survivor against this risk, especially in the case of boys. Boys are socialized to turn their anger and aggression outwards, so male victims may tend to victimize others while female victims are more likely to turn the anger in on themselves, by cutting or poisoning or starving themselves.

Instead of focusing on the unknown number of abuse victims who become abusers, it would be more profitable to study the much greater numbers of victims who do not abuse, and elucidate the ways in which they have achieved an altruistic and protective attitude towards children despite their own victimization. This research has yet to be undertaken.

Young men and children who abuse

Abuse is damaging whether the abuser is young or old, but age differences among abusers have important implications for treatment and prevention.

Children as young as five have been known to molest younger children sexually. At this stage it is better defined as 'acting out' than as abuse, but abnormal behaviour should be recognized and taken seriously, and the origins of the behaviour explored, not minimized as play or exploration.[21] Ten years on, the same boy may be well on the way to becoming a rapist, and may already be victimizing many younger children.

A 1992 survey by the National Children's Home suggested that a third of abusers are under eighteen, some living in a culture of abuse in which such behaviour is seen as the norm.

Unfortunately this adolescent abuse has too often been dismissed as 'part of growing up' or 'sexual experimentation', and no action taken. This is deeply negligent, overlooking the needs of both victim and abuser. It minimizes the harm done to victims and their need for help and healing, and it also dismisses the young person's last and only chance to grow into a happy normal adulthood.

Another danger is that in attributing abuse to less blame-worthy individuals, the true perpetrators once again adroitly avoid responsibility. I attended a conference in 1992 where a prison chaplain announced to me that a lot of csa is sibling abuse – adolescent experimentation. He seemed to think that this phenomenon was less serious than abuse by adults, and he had clearly not asked himself where such behaviour had come from in the first place. I doubt if he would have been happy for his own son to 'experiment' in this way. I was also disturbed at the way he used this argument to move the spotlight away from the responsibility of adult abusers.

Abusing behaviour becomes entrenched with repetition. The effectiveness of offender treatment programmes declines with offender age. The young abuser, if given help, has a good chance to change. As well as children's rights to be protected from abuse, we should not forget children's sacred right to be helped not to become abusers. Such treatment costs money. If the social will to provide it is not there (and at the moment it is not), we fail our children unforgivably.

There is an embarrassed tendency to gloss over incidents that may convey vital information about children at risk of developing abusive behaviour. In a recent case that I heard about, a four-year-old girl was hurt by her playmate, a six-year-old boy who cut her clitoris with scissors. The boy's parents dismissed it as simple naughtiness. The girl's mother agonized over whether to take the matter further, more worried about the boy than about her own child who made a good recovery. When she did report it to the NSPCC and they made a low-key, gentle investigation, the boy's parents were outraged. An otherwise responsible, intelligent couple respected in their community, they were unable to recognize their child's possible need for help or consider objectively whether someone might have initiated him into such behaviour.

It is more natural and easy to deny horrible possibilities than to confront them. People who do have the courage to confront their children's deviant behaviour often face isolation and criticism. Christine McGovern, founder of the organization

'Someone Cares', voices the anguish of a mother who did her best to bring her children up as loving, fulfilled people, only to find that her son (abused by an uncle at the age of ten) had at seventeen abused two younger children whom he was baby-sitting. She condemns her son's behaviour and accepted his custodial sentence – indeed she wanted him 'out of harm's way' until he had received effective treatment to stop the abuse. However, she could not accept the lack of treatment available in the young offenders' institution to which he was sent, and the lack of support and understanding for her own family in their ordeal. Instead of doing nothing, Christine founded a national campaign to call for more effective treatment for adolescent abusers and to provide self-help groups for their families.

She stands at the point where the pain of victims meets the pain of abusers' families. At her own son's trial his defence lawyer used the cheap tactic of smearing the child victims, saying one was provocative in her behaviour. Christine stood up and denounced him: 'How dare you say that? Them bairns was innocent!' For her, loving and caring for her abusing son did not include minimizing his crime or blaming his victims.

Christine has spoken about her own childhood abuse, abuse in her wider family, and her determination that the damage should now stop. She has been welcomed into several penal establishments and has set up support groups for offenders' families. She is one of the women whose ministry, costly and painful, shines out as a possibility of change in a situation of damage and despair. The Christian churches would benefit from recognizing and blessing such ministries.

Older abusers

Very few generalizations can be made about the characteristics of abusers. A decade ago it used to be said that they tended to be weak men, domestic tyrants ineffectual in the wider world. As more child sexual abuse has come to light and a greater variety has emerged, it is clear that there are no typical abusers; or to put it another way abusers are 'normal men'. They are not confined to one class, race or occupation. Parks

outlines one type of abuser who might be found in the Church
– the misogynous father:

> A high percentage of such offenders come from authori-
> tarian backgrounds with rigid or extreme controls, such
> as police work, the clergy or the armed forces . . .
> Children do not normally question obedience to an
> authoritarian father and have no illusions of mother
> being able to help or support them. Offenders within this
> category may be highly respected within the community,
> which isolates the child even more – few children feel
> they will be believed if their abuser is a policeman, the
> vicar or a pillar of the community.[22]

Although there is no 'typical abuser', there are characteristics
of abuser behaviour, and perhaps the most problematic are
secrecy and recidivism.

Intrafamilial abuse commonly continues for years. Abusers
are adept at maintaining secrecy, plausibility, the ability to
lead a double life. This is the characteristic that shows the
young child that the abuser knows what he is doing is wrong,
and by which he draws her into complicity which in turn
wreaks damage – 'I didn't tell anyone, so I must have allowed
it to happen.' Even the youngest children understand that if
they are pressed to keep something secret from those closest to
them it must be wrong. Their confusion over the two conflicting realities they must hold in their heads, the loving caretaker
and the abuser, threatens their sanity.

Secrecy facilitates the continuation of abuse. Child sexual
abuse is commonly described as a compulsive or addictive
behaviour; the terminology is a matter of clinical debate, but
the effect is the same. The child molester does not stop, even
when he is found out. Many will abuse any child to whom they
have access, opportunistically. The comparison with alco-
holism is a useful aid to understanding how compulsive this
behaviour is. To the non-abusing population, it may seem a
relatively simple matter for the abuser to cast off his perversion
and adjust to normality. In fact it is much harder for him to do
this than for the alcoholic to give up drink. Steven Wolf, an
American offenders' treatment expert, describes the offending
cycle:

[the offender] learns to protect himself through a variety of intellectual gymnastics. For example, after completing his sexual abuse (and this is especially true if he has just ejaculated) he is filled with guilt and remorse and promises to 'never do it again'. At that moment, the offender believes his promise. He fails to recognize that he has made this same promise repeatedly in the past. For the offender, every day is a new one. Not surprisingly, sexual offenders frequently have histories of active abuse behaviour which extend back many years and include multiple victims . . . This pattern of attraction, arousal, abuse, guilt, promises to stop, and back to attraction, is predictably present in nearly all sexual offenders . . . The offender is either unable or unwilling to recognize this repetitive quality in his past behaviour and, as a result, makes consistently wrong predictions about his future behaviour and his ability to control it.[23]

This has implications for Christian ministers who may be counsellors or confessors to abusers, or may be involved in helping their families. They must be realistic about the abuser's intentions to stop, and the prospects of his being safely reintegrated into the family.

Abusers rarely give up abusing. This is one of the truths so grim that we do not want to hear it. It is more hopeful to believe that a few months of therapy will do the trick and the happy family can be safely reunited. It is children who pay the price of this belief. It also fails to address the plight of abusers. We should not underestimate the demand we make of the abuser: to give up his main source of delight and pleasure, forswear the company of children, and lead a grey and bleak existence. However much we hate the abuse, we should not forget that giving it up is a heroic act. If it were easy to turn away from child molesting, more people would do it. In admitting the difficulty, however, we must never fall into the trap of minimizing the harm done.

Uncertain though the outcome is at present, treatment programmes for sex offenders are being researched and developed, and there is evidence that some offenders have been helped to change their behaviour.[24] Until more effective treatment is available, however, society is left with the dilemma of how to protect children from known abusers who have not been charged, or who have left prison. In October 1992 a British judge condemned a local council for leaving an abuser untreated in the community, because treatment would be too expensive.

Popular stereotypes of sex abusers provide camouflage for real abusers. They are often seen as sinister, cold, repellent and aggressive; whereas they are more likely to be charming, gentle, good with children, sympathetic and warm. Some of the hurdles of disbelief most people find it difficult to surmount are:

- I don't know anyone who abuses children.
- None of my friends would do that.
- No one in my family would do that.

It is a useful exercise to reflect on the fact that if you have several dozen friends and family members, it is statistically probable that at least one of them is a child-molester. What would you do if he or she were arrested for child abuse? Deny it, disbelieve it, ostracize him or her; or would you be able to help your friend to seek help with the problem?

In social terms, the natural tendency to believe that none of your friends is an abuser is disastrous for children. All abusers have friends (many are socially successful and extremely manipulative), and the wave of indignation and sympathy for the person accused of abuse can block any effective action to protect the child. It can even become (as in Cleveland in 1987) a political bandwagon crushing the rights of dozens of children and rendering the child-protective agencies powerless.

A realistic willingness to accept that some adults may be dangerous is often portrayed as paranoia. Some years ago a couple allowed their teenage son to go on a train-spotting trip to York with a friend, a middle-aged unmarried man who loved trains and railways and often took boys on similar weekends. A friend of the parent raised a casual question about the safety of such an arrangement. They turned on her. How could she be so dirty minded? Why did such a disgusting possibility occur to her?

The train enthusiast subsequently served a long prison sentence for abusing boys over many years.

This rallying to the defence of adults is always seen as natural and right, while discussing safeguards for children against a known hazard is seen as obsessive and unhealthy. There is a common lament that it is not even acceptable to smile at strange children and chat to them. Yet why should we be encouraging children to trust unknown adults? How can we expect them to distinguish between the harmless adult and the dangerous one, since we adults cannot? It should be considered sensible, rather than anti-social, to err on the side of caution.

Institutional abuse

Another much headlined problem which causes panic and dismay, despite its predictability, is the sad fact that child sexual abuse happens in institutions provided for the protection and welfare of children, such as schools and children's homes. My home town, Stockton-on-Tees, does not have an above average rate of child abuse, yet at the time of writing, a teacher at the local secondary school is on trial for sexually abusing pupils, and the former head of care at the local children's home has just received a heavy prison sentence for sexually abusing children in his care over many years:

> Bachelor Christopher Oldfield ruled with a rod of iron . . . The former soldier would hit the youngsters with his fists, according to police. He also used the cane . . . But behind the stern disciplined mask was a sinister, corrupt and sexually deviant mind. For five years the public-school-educated social worker subjected children in his care to a sustained period of sexual abuse. His youngest victim was a tragic six years old.[25]

Such depressing incidents elicit a complex range of reactions, often unhelpful. Among non-abusing adults they give rise to:

- Despair. If hurt and vulnerable children, subject to the

whole panoply of state provision, can be abused at the core of that system, they can never be protected.

• Apathy. They are children with multiple problems, this is just another one.

• Distancing. There is nothing I can do about it. I'll look after my own family and close my eyes to the pain I cannot remedy.

Abusing adults make political capital out of the same incidents. A man whose own children have been removed from home following sexual abuse by him will delight in pointing out that children are abused by the system that purports to protect them.

And yet it is obvious that there is no one-hundred-per-cent certain method of ensuring children's inviolability. Occupations involving contact with children (and this includes occupations within the Church) will always attract two kinds of people, among others: dedicated, caring, non-abusing adults, and predatory paedophiles. A man who wants access to children may well take a job as a teacher, nurse, social worker, school auxiliary, etc. It is unrealistic to expect that paedophiles could be excluded from such occupations, since there is no way (barring a previous conviction) of identifying them. Having accepted that, what is a responsible way forward? We need to find ways of strengthening the non-abusing parts of the family, church or institution, and establishing an atmosphere of openness in which it is more difficult for an oppressive regime to be maintained. In recent years NAYPIC (the National Association of Young People in Care) has been pressing for higher standards and more monitoring of residential children's homes. The chairperson of a 1992 official inquiry into the selection and support of staff in residential homes condemned social apathy towards this vulnerable client group and their carers:

> There's an amazing amount of wishful thinking and fatalism about children's homes. Some people seem to be operating on the assumption that abuse can't happen there. Or if it does, then nothing can be done about it.[26]

Abuse of children with disabilities

Confronting this problem has been called 'thinking the un-
thinkable'. Marchant[27] lists the myths we use to defend
ourselves against the knowledge that children with disabilities
are abused:

1. 'Disabled children are less vulnerable to abuse.' (*Untrue.*
They may be protected from 'stranger danger' but they are
vulnerable to abuse by carers. We assume they are respected
and protected, but this is not always so. Their powerlessness
may make them particularly attractive to an abuser.)

2. 'Sexual abuse of disabled children is not very harmful.'
(*Untrue.* The betrayal of trust, to a person dependent on loving
carers, is devastating. Abused children feel dirty, guilty,
frightened and depressed. Their prospects of a happy sexual
relationship in adulthood are severely affected.)

3. 'Preventing the abuse of disabled children is too difficult.'
(This is *unacceptable.* Children with disabilities have enough
problems to face without this one as well – they have a right to
be protected from it. They can be helped to be assertive and
confident.)

4. 'Children with learning difficulties invent incidents of
abuse.' (*Almost never true.* False allegations are extremely rare.
Children disclose abuse with reluctance and embarrassment.)

5. 'It is harmful to address the problem, once abuse has
happened. Best leave well alone.' (*Untrue.* All children,
including those with disabilities, benefit from being heard,
believed and supported. Their physical and mental health
throughout their lives may be affected if this does not happen.
Psychotherapy could and should be provided for sexually
abused children with disabilities.[28])

Child sexual abuse and other social problems

It is important to be aware of the interconnectedness of abuse with other problems, for example homelessness. A survey by CHAR (Campaign for Homeless People) found that over 40 per cent of homeless girls were fleeing from sexual abuse, often to end up on the streets.[29] Many commentators feel that the CHAR survey, though an admirable piece of work, under-estimates the problem. A housing association worker suggested to me that 80 per cent was a more likely figure.

An associated problem is prostitution. Children who run away from home are sometimes forced by poverty to sell sexual services.

A proportion of teenage pregnancies are the result of csa. Doctors are recommended to consider the possibility of csa in any pregnant young teenager where the baby's father is not known.[30]

Is abuse really a problem in the Church?

The short answer is that there is no reason to think that the rate of child sexual abuse is any lower within the Church than outside it. In fact there is some evidence from the United States to suggest a higher than expected number of churchgoers among child abusers:

> The majority of reported aggressors are regular church attenders. It is difficult to measure someone's 'Christianity', but researchers do report that the adult males [male abusers] tend to be very devout, moralistic and conservative in their religious beliefs.[31]

Summary

- Child sexual abuse involves an adult using a child for the adult's sexual gratification.

- At least one in ten children suffer sexual abuse, the majority within their own family or immediate circle. Sexual abuse is almost always characterized by enforced secrecy and silencing based on affection, authority, violence or threats.
- The harm done often results in severe physical and mental symptoms at the time of the abuse and in later life.
- Abusers can be any age, occupation, social class, race or religion. Over 90 per cent of abusers are male.
- Victims are both male and female children – probably in roughly equal numbers among young children, but greater numbers of girls than boys as children get older.
- Young abusers have the greatest chance of changing their behaviour, if the right intervention is offered.
- Adult abusers are rarely 'cured', and any child to whom they have access must be considered at risk. If a child is being sexually abused within the family, other children within that family are also at risk.
- You know at least one child – more likely several – who is suffering sexual abuse.
- You probably know at least one person who is a child-molester.
- Paedophiles will place themselves, often with great skill, in a position to have access to children, whether in families or in institutions. This is not a reason to dismantle either families or state child-care provision, but it is a political and ethical challenge to society to make them safe for children.
- It is likely that the rate of child sexual abuse within Christian communities is similar to the rate in the non-Christian population.
- Abuse survivors, like abusers, are found in all walks of life and all occupations. Many Christian ministers are abuse survivors.

3

Responses

How does the Church respond when faced with sexually abused children, or when abuse survivors turn to their Church for help? Some survivors encounter sympathy and support; others meet only suspicion, horror or ignorance. It seems to depend to a great extent on the sensitivity and awareness of individual ministers and church members.

Responses to adult survivors of child sexual abuse

I asked members of two Christian survivors' groups about their experiences; these are some of their replies:

■ The church I am a member of was a great support to me (an Anglican, middle-of-the-road, liberal-thinking church). Most people, clergy and lay, are understanding, but I have found one or two people who had no understanding of the effects of child sexual abuse, and it was obvious they had their own emotional difficulties with it.

■ It is wrong to assume that all clergy are capable of dealing with survivors of child sexual abuse. There is still a need for more training. I have found that people from fundamentalist Christian churches have the most difficulty in feeling accepted.

Christian survivors often stress that their personal relationship with God is a source of help and strength, but their church is not:

■ I found faith in Jesus Christ very helpful. However I found that people were generally very misinformed about sexual abuse, and many found the subject very distressing, leading them in turn to abuse me mentally or spiritually. I have found Christianity very helpful, but this was through my relationship with God, not theirs.

■ God doesn't rationalize and lay guilt at your own door. I found it comforting to bring my abuse to him and leave it there.

■ I know God is with me, for me, there; certainly knows my lot, knows the suffering, knows the pain, hurt, loneliness. Yes. I know God knows me. I feel his presence. He's my lifelong friend. He has placed some wonderful people in my path. I consider my therapist a gift from God. My faith has been very important – but it's a *personal* faith, just God and me. I love communion. I love the Mass. Outside that the church is meaningless. The priesthood (all male) irks me, hurts me, offends me.

■ Jesus was a victim, he too suffered deep pain, vulnerability and powerlessness. However, I only benefited from this understanding once I had worked out a lot of negative emotions in psychotherapy.

Christian survivors' support groups were a valued source of help:

■ I heard about Safety Net [a London-based Christian survivors' group] and went along. People there had been helped by counselling. I began to realize that beneath my bold exterior there were many hurts and doubts to be dealt with.

Others, who did not have access to a survivors' support group, had found help and acceptance from individual survivors:

■ Some Christians were extremely supportive, mostly those who had gone through the same experience as me. They offered support, a caring time to listen, prayers, and healing – God's unconditional love. They showed me God on the side of the survivor.

People with no experience of the problem were nevertheless helpful if they were able to listen to and respect the experience of the abused person:

■ Two priests I know were wonderful, but I think this was because they were the people they were, rather than because they were priests. Priesthood doesn't seem to affect the bad ones, who are insensitive or simplistic ('Pray about it, my dear'). These two were patient, non-judgemental. They listened. They knew the issues were complex, and they did not try to 'play God'. They knew they didn't understand, were not experts, and didn't try to give advice – because they instinctively knew advice after my experiences was hollow and meaningless. I felt their respect. They knew I was the 'expert' but needed support and encouragement. They didn't try to cure me, heal me, they simply stayed with me.

■ As someone who became a Christian in the evangelical wing of the church, my faith now finds greatest expression in the catholic wing, mainly because there is no attempt to ignore, minimize or offer pat answers over issues of suffering and doubt.

■ My Christian friends cared for me even when I was full of doubt and deeply depressed.

A feeling of safety was another key factor:

■ The important thing is that one has to feel safe to be more open to others. In that way I have found much love, help and acceptance.

Some survivors felt that their churches were willing to help, but hampered by fear, distress or lack of understanding:

■ Education and training is needed for people who want to start facing these issues (survivors and helpers).

■ I am wary about coming out as a survivor in any kind of Christian context. When I spoke to the Diocesan Children's Committee, they were very open and supportive but still I found I was reading my story as if it had happened to somebody else. I still have this feeling that it will be held against me, anything I say thereafter will be discounted as either neurotic or obsessive, and I find that worrying. I'm afraid of being blamed for raising this unpleasant issue. I seem to get either the 'There, there, tut, tut, have a paper hanky (but don't tell me anything more about it!)' approach, or else *I* end up consoling *them*. I tend to watch out for signs that it's OK to tell someone, and recently I've opened up a bit more to people in the church who I think might be accepting, because I feel very strongly that the issue needs to be raised in the church. I've recently told two Catholic priests. In both cases I found myself comforting them – one just sat there with his head in his hands, and I felt as if I'd hurt him by telling him. The other one ended up in tears, so that left me doing the 'There, there' bit. I'd got my courage up to tell them, but they didn't really see me at all, just their own upset. I found it very nerve-racking telling them, and it was bizarre to find myself comforting them.

Some survivors had found little if any help in their churches. The all-male clergy were mentioned as a problem by several:

■ I found it hard to trust authority figures like clergy, and deliberately avoided telling them about my abuse.

Images of a powerful God were also painful:

■ How can I trust a powerful authority figure like God? How can I be angry with God?

Counselling, if offered, was often inappropriate:

■ The Christian counselling I initially received was directive, it did not allow space for expression of grief, fury and betrayal, and gave no space to explore my perceptions of God.

■ Some priests are not helpful. I was told once to go to confession to confess my sins of impurity. When I told one priest I was an abuse survivor he told me not to look back. He said to remember Lot's wife – she looked back and was turned into a pillar of salt. . . .

I don't know how I've managed to stay a (Catholic) Christian. I think it's largely God's doing, not letting humans undermine my picture – His picture – of love, care, respect. Unfortunately too many Christians profess to know the answers. I keep quiet where 'answers' are concerned. In child abuse there are rarely answers/solutions/explanations. One just needs a *safe* love – not love that exploits. (I was sexually assaulted by a vicar.)

Why do so many in the Church judge and pontificate when we should stay quiet? Many times we simply do not know how to help and support the survivor. The advice to listen, believe, support and respect seems paltry, not enough. If only Christians would not set out to heal/cure/do something. These end up harming. So many times when I've been in pain I've been told to pray – as if I don't! 'Pray – since you're obviously not praying' seems to be the message. This Christmas I got a novena on a Christmas card which is designed to take away the pain! [A novena is a Catholic 'nine-day prayer'.] Simplistic formulas are not enough, advice to put it behind you, it's in the past – pat, meaningless remarks. I'd rather hear 'Yes, you bloody well do hurt, yes, you bloody well are angry – that's OK – you were betrayed.' I have a very deep conviction that God/Jesus is angry and hurt along with me. Jesus is bloody angry. He didn't smash up the Temple for nothing. We Christians do not get angry enough. We want peace and joy when in fact good old anger might help *a lot* of survivors. Forgiveness is another area that needs to be explored. Simple pat answers appear again: 'Forgive – you are a Christian' – but there's no recognition of the real difficulty and complexity of forgiveness.

This eloquent analysis uncovers the source of well-meaning, unhelpful counsel. Christianity is supposed to be about goodness, charity, caring, mediating the love of God. It is hard for Christians to 'stay quiet' when they feel there must be a correct formula for helping.

Blaming the victim?

Christian denominations with a more active pastoral tradition are more likely to have developed a systematic response. The advantage of this is that the survivor will normally be accepted and counselled; the disadvantage is that the counselling may be inappropriate, or based on an approach which the survivor experiences as offensive and demeaning.

Jackie, a survivor living in Tyneside, went with a friend to a day course on 'Helping survivors of child sexual abuse', held at a local Baptist church. This is her account of it:

■ I'm not a Christian, but I was open to the idea that it might have something helpful to offer. We were taken aback by the hymns and prayers at the beginning of the day – talking about God as Father, and 'Him' and 'His power'. If you've been on the receiving end of abusive power, you may not want to sing about the power and glory of God.

The basic information they gave about child sexual abuse was quite good, but they seemed to move on quickly to their main focus, which was the sinfulness of abuse survivors. All right, they weren't blaming the victim for the actual abuse but they seemed to see the victim as culpable afterwards. I know Christians think everyone is sinful, so they could justify it logically in that sense, but why was the overwhelming emphasis on the guilt of the victim/survivor?

The main speaker was an abuse survivor. What she was saying was that the person who has been abused goes on to abuse, not sexually but in the sense that they often abuse the person who is counselling them. Because the survivor is needy, she demands and takes too much, is too draining – and until the survivor sees that she is taking too much from other people she can't possibly be healed.

She went on and on about this – that abuse survivors need other people's time and attention so much, they just take,

take, take, and that is not a basis for a proper fellowship, it is one-sided. They must be counselled to accept that they are guilty of this *further sin*. Until Christian counsellors could make these people realize that they were sinners and that their sin was to demand too much, there was no hope for them.

The structure of the day was such that it was difficult to challenge this stuff. I felt very intimidated. I wish I had found the courage to stand up and say 'Hey, you lot, what on earth are you talking about?' I did confront one of the speakers later, one to one, and he tried to justify it by saying that we are all sinners, none of us are perfect in the eyes of God.

Jackie was alarmed by the possible consequences of such an approach for vulnerable Christian abuse survivors:

■   I'm not a Christian, I don't know that I can accept there is a God of any sort, but for someone who actually believes in God, to seek help and then get that sort of rubbish talked at them, I don't know how they would survive. In the audience at this course, there were presumably some survivors hearing these messages . . . and probably some abusers, too, happily noting that the main blame seemed to be falling on abused people.

Healing was to come from Jesus. That was the message – Jesus as the instant fix. Take him into your heart and you're OK. For people with deep-seated and painful problems it must be a tempting option, short-circuiting the pain and confusion.

The big theme of the day was the idea of shame, inappropriate shame leading to various shortcomings. It was explained this way: survivors feel lacking, can't cope with exposure, and this becomes a problem for society! You can't bear shame and therefore turn it into contempt. As a child, you are a victim, but as an adult you become an 'abusing agent' – that's the phrase they used – because of what happened to you. 'You're selfish and greedy, because you're a mess and you're needy.' You harm others by wanting too much from them. You perpetuate the damage to yourself by the need to be needed. The emphasis was always, your need is so great, you shouldn't look to other humans to satisfy that need, you should look to God, throw yourself on God and you will be healed.

Now, it depends on your own perception, but I don't believe you can be healed of the abuse. You can survive, but you never fully recover. I can relate to the image of being on a journey – there are stages in the journey and you begin to perceive yourself differently. But it is not healing. You cannot recover a lost childhood. The damage done cannot be undone. You will always be affected by it. What changes is the way in which you allow it to affect you. When I first became aware of my abuse, I just went to pieces, fell into a whimpering heap on the floor. My way of dealing with it has changed, but what happened cannot change. The only thing that changes is that with time I become more and more aware of what happened.

According to this speaker, however, you have to be healed. The process of healing, she said, starts with getting rid of this shame. Survivors have to repent of 'the harm they have done to themselves and others'. This is what you have to sorrow over – not the loss of your childhood, or the hurt inner child, but the annoyance of others!

She said that survivors have to realize that their way of relating has harmed themselves and others because of their neediness and incapacity to give. She didn't seem to think that someone who has been a victim is actually capable of giving. I felt that was ignorant and insulting, seeing people who have been abused as recipients and obedient counsellees, rather than people with their own wisdom and contribution to offer.

She insisted on the willingness to forgive. The only way you can be healed is to forgive those who harmed you. There was no mention of expressing anger; the only way to come to God was to forgive, 'pursuing love and eschewing revenge, desiring restoration of the abuser'. You are supposed to say to your abuser, 'You have done me harm, but I want to pursue you in love for your sake.'

Another way in which survivors are seen as sinful is that they commonly become involved in 'immoral relationships', which seems to include everything from premarital sex to lesbian relationships. You are supposed to repent of that as well.

I think that what really frightened me was that most of those folk there would go away from that study day feeling 'Right, I know how to deal with abuse victims.' They feel they have the answers. There's no sense of the individual. No doubt some survivors fit their stereotype (very few I'd think), but it was such a stock approach: 'This is how you deal with a sexual abuse victim.'

It may be only one of many Christian approaches, but what worries me is that many abused people may be drawn to this proffered ministry, and may be irreparably harmed by it. If they'd been trying to counsel me, for example, three years ago, I would have landed up back in a psychiatric ward, for ever probably, because on top of everything else I'd have been feeling like a terrible sinner. Now, I can laugh at it, but for someone at the beginning of awareness of their abuse it could be as damaging as not doing anything at all, if not more so.

This day-course, Jackie later discovered, was based on a system of Bible-based counselling which has become very influential in some Christian circles in the USA and Britain. It was developed by Dr Larry Crabb, and is described in an eloquent book by Dan B. Allender, *The Wounded Heart*.[1] Since many survivors will encounter this kind of Christian counselling, it is worth looking more closely at this book.

It is an admirable work in many ways, a sensitive and skilled analysis of what sexual abuse is and feels like, how it is planned and carried out, and an uncompromising definition of abuse, which does not condone the idea that 'lesser' forms of abuse are less harmful:

> . . . *all inappropriate sexual contact is damaging and soul-distorting.* Seventy-four per cent of the least severely-abused victims report severe damage later in life . . . Verbal abuse is a powerful and deep wound. *Sexually abusive words produce the same damage as sexually abusive contact.* Yet the potential for minimization or feeling weird for being damaged makes the potential for change even more difficult for those more subtly abused than for those more severely abused. [emphasis in original][2]

Allender warns against the temptations of the 'quick fix', and recognizes the dangers inherent in the abused person's search for an all-powerful authority figure to heal her:

The abused person often looks for someone who is strong, authoritative and convinced that the damage can be quickly and painlessly resolved . . . Quick cures never resolve the deep damage . . . There are many options available to the Christian for dealing with past abuse, but the outcome is unappealing: forgive and forget – denial; pressured love – passionless conformity; quick cures – irresponsible passivity. It is not difficult to understand why the Christian who has been abused often chooses either to seek help outside the church or to learn to handle the damage by pretending it does not exist.[3]

However, after this excellent introductory groundwork, Allender goes on to the more dubious part of his analysis: the problem of shame. This syndrome includes defensiveness, coldness, inability to be open and vulnerable; traits generally recognized as typical sequelae of abuse. Allender accurately identifies the process: being hurt so badly that you never again open yourself up to the vulnerability of love, and carrying a load of inappropriate guilt which leads to a nagging sense of shame. Feelings of shame and guilt are common responses to abuse, and torment abuse survivors until they are dealt with appropriately. Allender's terminology and emphases, however, are problematic. He says that the abused person is her own enemy:

The enemy is sin, that fallen, autonomous striving for life that refuses to bow to God. *The enemy is the internal reality that will not cry out to God in humble, broken dependence.* It is the victim's subtle or blatant determination to make life work on her own by refusing to acknowledge or let God fulfil her deepest longing.[4] [emphasis in original]

It seems inappropriate to recommend 'humble, broken dependence' to a person whose childhood experience of humble, broken dependence was a living hell. It is also questionable to condemn the survivor's defences as 'her enemy'. Her hard shell may be her enemy now but it was her good friend in the past, helping her to block out the horror and survive. It is too simple to condemn it as 'sin'.

Allender's emphasis is wrong in focusing on the survivor's

sinfulness as her main enemy. He says his intention in this is good, in that she can deal with her own sinfulness whereas she is powerless to deal with the abuser, but the effect, as Jackie found attending the day-course based on this model, is that the focus is relentlessly on the sinfulness of the victim. This begins to sound much too close to the abuser's own ploy of blaming the victim.

In the end an approach which highlights the sins of the victim cannot be a useful starting-point for healing. Allender's approach also denies the healing that comes via other channels:

> The solution the secular path offers is in fact filling a leaky cup with lukewarm water. It leaves the soul empty and unsatisfied. It never admits that the deepest damage is never what someone has done to me but what I have done regarding the Creator of the universe.[5]

Many Christians would disagree with this, and many have been helped by secular therapists. One survivor who wrote to me described her (non-Christian) therapist as a gift from God.

This is not intended as a blanket criticism of evangelical Christianity. Many Christian survivors have encountered their first experience of love and healing in an evangelical setting. Non-Christians may be dubious about the value of being 'born again' as a means of healing; but the symbolism of rebirth is highly efficacious for some victims, a powerful source of consolation for a destroyed childhood.

■ I believe in Jesus Christ as someone alive, not dead, from whom you can seek assistance. I was then acquainted with a whole new community of young Christians, many of whom had been in similar situations . . . I believe that my faith in Jesus Christ has helped me to overcome my difficulties . . . What is so good about this Christian group is that everyone is regarded as equal. At school, I had terrible problems about looking Chinese; other kids called me names. Besides, I felt bad about looking Chinese because my father is Chinese. I hated Chinese men. I wanted to look white like the others. Here, among our Christian group, I feel part of a community. I feel more confident about myself . . . I would now like to help others to overcome these difficulties.[6]

This young woman speaks of Christianity as a route to self-affirmation, self-love leading to a desire to help others. The solidarity of her Christian community, and the fact that many of them are also abuse survivors, is vital to her.

With some evangelical groups, however, where the love and care available may be insufficient to help with the damage of abuse, there is a danger that psychologically hurt and vulnerable people may be attracted to the group, only to feel even more let down and emotionally frozen when they discover the limits of the fellowship on offer.

This is often the case with those groups that foster negative assumptions about homosexuality. Jackie mentioned the disapproval of lesbianism, and it is all too common to find homosexuality listed as one of the ill-effects of abuse. A survivor quoted by Robertson says:

■ . . . sometime between the ages of ten and twelve, my father started abusing me . . . [Later on] I was lured into a brief lesbian friendship. I'm told that this is another result of having been abused as a child.[7]

Allender and similar writers seem to accept without discussion the proposition that homosexuality is both dysfunctional and one of the harmful consequences of sexual abuse. This is needlessly insulting and insensitive to homosexual women and men, and lumps in what many Christians see as one of God's greatest gifts (their capacity of self-giving and self-fulfilment through human love) with the evil consequences resulting from sexual abuse.

This is not the place to discuss the genesis of sexual orientation, or pursue the debate about it current in the Christian church. It may be that women who have a potential to relate sexually to either sex and have known only abusive treatment from men, may choose to express their sexuality with women. It is certainly the case that the proportion of the population affected by child sexual abuse overlaps with the substantial proportion who know themselves to be homosexual, but it would be difficult to elicit any causal relationship. It is unjustifiable to label homosexuality as part of the damage done by abuse, when many women and men experience it as a source of love and healing. Abuse survivors have quite enough to cope with without attacks upon aspects of their nature which they feel to be God-given and good; such attacks only obscure the real damage they have suffered.

Responses to children

If the Christian Church does not always respond helpfully to adult survivors of csa, how does it respond when there is reason to believe that a child is being molested? This concern will not be raised frequently, since most csa is kept secret, but when a case does arise the pastoral response should be sensitive and child-centred.

A minister may become involved because the family turns to him for help. In the case of suspected intrafamilial abuse, there is a particular hazard. The minister who is not sufficiently experienced or informed may perceive not a child at risk and a family with various needs and problems, but a family threatened with break-up by callous professionals. He may be particularly susceptible, as a caring helper, to the distress and protestations of innocence of an abusing father. The result may be (and this is hard to excuse) that the minister becomes aligned with the abuser against the child victim, and the moral authority of the Church seemingly reinforces the abuser's denunciations of interfering professionals.

What may lead a priest into this catastrophic situation? Perhaps it is the scope of clergy training, which includes a wide swathe of skills of various kinds, some better apprehended than others. Perhaps it is due to the churches' search for relevance, for a leading role within the community.

In 1989 I spoke with an Anglican priest who had aligned himself very publicly and influentially with the 'innocent parents' of children in whom there was a serious concern of sexual abuse. His support for the parents who denied the possibility of abuse had helped to fuel a media campaign which disrupted the joint investigation procedures and eventually resulted in most of the children being returned home with the concern of abuse unresolved.[8] I asked him why he had decided to take such a partisan line. Should he not have offered pastoral care for the people involved without expressing an opinion on whether the children had been abused or not? What had convinced him the children were not being abused, when so many child-care professionals had found grave cause for concern? He answered that he had done a lot of work in counselling grieving children, and he was experienced in recognizing grief. If the children had suffered that kind of trauma, he would have perceived it.

In fact there are no such convenient markers to indicate that sexual abuse is happening. All authorities agree that children suffering csa can and often do maintain an appearance of absolute normality, frequently by 'splitting off' the abusive parts of their lives and screening them out from the 'normal' part. The priest's experience, and assumption of his own expertise, led him to an unjustified conclusion. Perhaps more disturbing is the fact that he wielded such power and influence in this situation without the necessary professional responsibility or training. He was asked in a public inquiry – too late to undo the damage – if he had considered that some of the children had in fact been abused. He replied, 'I have not tried in depth to look critically. I have not seen that as my role.'[9]

Why do the churches seem to find it hard to respond protectively to abused children? Elizabeth and Susan (chapter 1) both disclosed their abuse in confession; both were disbelieved or ignored, and effectively silenced. (The seal of the confessional may prevent reporting of abuse, but it should not prevent a priest from counselling a child on how to seek help.)

Failure to respond in a child-centred way to abuse can lead to cruelty. In 1989 a twelve-year-old Irish girl was sexually abused by a friend of her father. The abuse continued over two years, culminating in full rape at the end of 1991. She became pregnant and suicidal.

For a child who has undergone such an ordeal, healing is difficult and slow. The people caring for her agreed that one prerequisite was that she should not be forced to bear a child to her rapist. However, in Ireland the Catholic Church has a strong influence on the State. The judiciary's reaction to the rape of this child was a draconian ban on any move to end the pregnancy.

This is not the place to recycle the entire debate about

abortion, but this was a case where even many conservative Christians felt it would be justifiable. Lawyers for the child argued that the risk to her own life was substantial, as she had already threatened suicide. The judge ruled against this plea, arguing that since the girl was living with caring parents, the risk of suicide was 'lessened'. In other words, the judiciary proposed testing a rape victim to destruction. Public outrage ensued and the decision was later overturned.

Interestingly, the strongest arguments against abortion are of the 'slippery slope' variety. Although we cannot say when human personhood begins, it is argued, unless human life is protected from the moment of conception, society's inherent selfish and inhumane tendencies will gradually devalue all human life. The Irish case showed up the flaw in this argument, which, in the name of avoiding hypothetical future inhumanity, insisted on the infliction of such suffering on an abused child.

Responses to abuse by clergy

Accounts of child-molesting by clergy are increasingly common. There is no reason to think that the clergy of any church do not include a certain number of child-molesters: some who have deliberately chosen their occupation so that they can have access to children, others with a genuine vocation but apparently unable to control their paedophilic behaviour. None of this should be surprising. The problem is made many times worse when a church seeks to deny or hide this fact; and the problem is not one of abstract injustice or hypocrisy, it is a criminal policy of putting further children at risk from known abusers.

This is the main theme in parents' complaints against the hierarchy in the latest spate of paedophile scandals in the Roman Catholic Church. They complain, not only that the church negligently put their children at risk, but that it deliberately exposed their children to known paedophiles, moving abusers from parish to parish every time abuse was exposed. Fr Anton Mowat (see chapter 1) was moved from England to the USA when the suspicion of child abuse arose, and from the USA to Italy when the same thing happened again. Fr Robert Mayer, a Chicago priest facing several child-molesting charges, was moved four times, each move following new allegations of abuse. Fr Gilbert Gauthe of Louisiana abused upwards of two hundred children over a period of five to seven years, and was moved from parish to parish in the same way.[10]

This used to be known as the 'geographical solution' and was the method of choice when dealing with child abusers. It seems to combine the worst of all possible solutions: it exposes the abuser to a constant supply of new victims, it offers no protection to them nor information to their parents, and it affords the abuser no incentive to stop – rather the opposite. Yet the Catholic Church seems to have kept on doing it until the sheer weight of lawsuits from the parents of the young victims made it impractical.

Even where a paedophile priest is made to leave parish work or the priesthood, this is usually done quietly and without charges being brought. He is sent forth into a community which does not have the necessary information to protect its children from him. Fr Dino Cinel (see chapter 1), who 'performed anal sex, group sex, oral sex and a dizzying array of other diversions with at least seven teenage boys', was quietly dismissed from his parish and left to pursue a lucrative career as a university professor. The Church made no move either to compensate his victims or to protect other children from him. One of the policemen involved in his case pointed out:

> Based on the lack of proof of rehabilitation other than Cinel saying 'I've given it up', I can only assume that what he's doing at the present time is molesting kids, because that's what Dino Cinel has always done, and everything else . . . has been secondary. If he's photographed seven boys, he's seduced seventy, and if he's seduced seventy, he's taken a shot at seven hundred.[11]

Two of Fr Cinel's victims are now suing the Church.

It is not as if this is a new problem which has taken the authorities by surprise. Jason Berry, author of a forthcoming book on priests and paedophilia, reports:

> Roughly $300 million has been paid by church officials and insurers since 1985 in cases of priests abusing children and adolescents . . . there have been at least 200 [American] priests or brothers reported to the Vatican Embassy for such offences in the last six years alone.[12]

The Catholic Church is suffering from a critical shortage of priests (partly self-inflicted, since it is one of the denominations that rejects the vocations of women). Could this be a contributory factor to the authorities' reluctance to take dangerous priests out of circulation?

Attitudes are changing, and the infamous 'geographical solution' is increasingly regarded as criminally negligent. Describing a case of abuse by a priest, Rossetti explains the responsibilities of the Church:

> Those parents reasonably relied on 'the church'. They entrusted their son to the priest in question not because they knew or trusted him personally . . . but because the priest was clothed in the moral authority of the institution he represented. Courts will often find that this 'reasonable reliance' on the part of innocent people is sufficient to find that an institution had a duty to protect innocent third parties from the misconduct of its agents.[13]

Legal considerations aside, the acid test of an ethical response to child sexual abuse is whether it is child-centred or adult-centred. The child-centred response puts the child's recovery, and the protection of children from abuse, at the top of its agenda, and all negotiations with adults are subordinate to that. Adult-centred responses hardly see the child, or they treat him as an embarrassment; they are concerned to resolve matters with minimum disruption. The Catholic Church, which should and could give a model of the healing, child-centred response even at the cost of some embarrassment to itself, seems automatically to adopt a classic adult-centred agenda. In doing so it does no service to abusive clergy, who are left with their problem unresolved, and it endangers further vulnerable children with whom the abusers will come into contact.

Repentance

The churches have a sorry record of failing abused children. One sign of hope in recent years is the message of Archbishop Alphonsus Penney of Newfoundland, who heard reports of child abuse by religious for fifteen years and took no action. When the scandal broke he did not take refuge in self-justification but resigned, saying to the abused youngsters and their fellow parishioners:

> We are a sinful Church . . . Our anger, our pain, our anguish, our shame and our vulnerability are clear to the whole world. . . . We are sorry for the times you were not believed, were not supported or were ostracised in any way by the community. For every word and action which has deepened your pain, we are profoundly sorry.[14]

The Archbishop's words and actions may become a source of healing for many who feel rejected or abused by their church. Following the Newfoundland scandal, the Canadian Bishops' Conference produced a report which set out resolutions for the future:

> We would like to see our Church guided by a spirit of openness and truth when responding to allegations of child sexual abuse by a priest or a religious . . . We would like to see our Church face, with clarity and courage, the decisions that must be taken in the light of the failure that child abuse represents for society and the Church itself.[15]

Will churches in Britain be guided by this ideal or repeat the same mistakes? It is hard to tell. In 1992–3 the RC Church faced a cluster of cases of csa by clergy, including Frs. Samuel Penney (Birmingham) and Anthony McAllan (Humberside). Fr. Penney abused children from several families over 25 years and was moved from parish to parish as concerns of abuse were raised.[16] Fr. McAllan abused boys in his cottage on Holy Island, a place of Christian pilgrimage.[17] His bishop expressed regret to the victims and determination to do all he could to ensure children's safety in his diocese.

4

'Crawling along a rough and painful road'

This chapter is not headed 'healing', because many survivors reject this term as inaccurate and misleading. A lost and ruined childhood cannot be retrospectively restored, with the damage undone. A foster mother who cares for very hurt children tells them: 'I can't take away the things that have happened to you, but I can share them. You may never recover completely, but you will learn to live with the scars just as you live with physical scars. Pain is part of life. Face yours, be honest about what you feel.'[1]

Children's pain

Facing the pain is an ordeal for adult survivors, and a terrible burden to lay on children. Most children carry the pain of abuse alone, and do not reveal it (if at all) until adulthood: 'Disclosure is not the norm, because the child's survival depends on the process of secrecy, helplessness, entrapment, delayed or conflicted disclosure and retraction.'[2]

Even in the case of children who try to escape abuse, there are very few routes open to them. Little children do not on the whole have access to child-care professionals who might be able to help them. Helen Armstrong, a trainer for the National Children's Bureau, carries out an exercise with study groups in which participants draw a star to represent an abused child. Marked points are drawn close to or further away from the child to represent adults with whom the child has contact and to whom she might be able to talk about things that distress her. Teachers are one possibility; ministers or church workers another. The exercise highlights children's lack of individual access to helping agencies, and the responsibility of agencies embedded in the community to be aware and trained to be helpful to children who need them.

Children whose abuse does come to light should, and usually will, be given support and healing, both through age-appropriate therapy for themselves and through support for the mother (or other non-abusing carer) who has a key role in the child's recovery.

> Skills in helping bereaved people, especially children, through the process of grief and mourning can be transferred to work with abused children. Mistreated youngsters have suffered a whole host of losses: of self esteem, of dignity, of security, of ability to trust, of unconditional parental love, of sibling companionship and of part of their childhood. Loss reactions can be seen in abused children and their siblings. Denial, guilt, anger, sleep disorders, repression, isolation and helplessness are among the emotional responses that the bereaved and the abused hold in common.
>
> Working with abused children requires emotional resilience. Some adults find the pain of the child unbearable.[3]

Often children are seen as passive objects, recipients of abuse, concern or therapy. It is easy to forget the courage and commitment they must show in order to 'unlearn' the abuse they have been taught. Psychotherapist Ann Alvarez speaks movingly of her child clients' lonely struggle towards normality, towards normal friendship and tenderness, when all they have known since babyhood has been the need to trade sexual services for affection.[4]

She tells the story of one six-year-old boy who had been

severely anally abused for years. On the way to his weekly visit to his psychotherapist, he and his social worker had bought some iced buns. He was telling his therapist about them, but the word 'bun' kept coming out as 'bum'. Try as he might, the hated memory was intruding. Any other six-year-old would have been giggling at such a slip, but this child was sobbing and distraught at his inability to exclude the unwanted thought.

Abused children, says Alvarez, have confronted the reality of evil at a very early age: 'Their rescuers have little to teach them about human evil, selfishness, greed and lust.' They may be very ill equipped to rebuild their lives. Early abuse may have disrupted their development so much that they have little sense of self. 'You need to have the sense of an intact self in order to feel outrage at being abused', says Alvarez. They may have to learn anger – not a traditional ingredient of Christian teaching. They have to face loss and grief, if the abuser was a parent. It is heart-rending to see a child going through these ordeals; but it is important to remember that healing and therapy provided at this stage – both directly to the child and indirectly through support of the non-abusing carer – offer the best chance of a good outcome. Provision of therapy for abused children is improving, and is undertaken both by the health and social services and by charities such as the National Society for the Prevention of Cruelty to Children and the National Children's Home.

Adult survivors: the recovery process

One of the adult survivors who rejects the term 'healing' is Dorothy, whose story is told in chapter 1. She describes the process as

■ . . . adjustment, rather than healing. I don't know about healing. If someone talks to me about it I feel panicky, as if they're asking me to jump to a place I'm nowhere near, and won't be for the foreseeable future. Some days I'm OK and other days it's dreadful. I feel as if I've climbed out of a slimy bog and I'm crawling along a rough and painful road. Sometimes I feel absolutely hopeless.

The abused person's first request for help may be timid and tentative. The response she receives is crucial, and may greatly help or hinder her struggle to survive. Hansen has produced a useful leaflet for priests and pastoral workers, advising them how to understand and respond to a first disclosure. She lists these priorities:

– *Believe the survivor*. She may have been disbelieved in the past. She may have trouble herself believing the horror of what she went through.

– *Take the abuse seriously*. The abuse may be in the past, but the trauma is in the present. Do not encourage the survivor to minimise the abuse. He may have very low self-esteem, feeling he does not matter, therefore what was done to him does not matter.

– *Tell the survivor it was not her fault*. She may feel to blame if she complied under threats or coercion, or was given money or sweets afterwards, or obeyed to try to protect a sibling from abuse. The abuser may have told her she 'made him do it'.

– *Tell the survivor he has done the right thing in telling you about it*. He may regret it, be overwhelmed with shame and guilt, or feel he has betrayed his abuser.[5]

Pastors should be aware of the need to refer on to an experienced therapist when the survivor feels ready. The 'rough road' she has to travel can be dangerous. The survivor can be beset with feelings of terrible despair and grief as she relives the abuse. Skilled support is necessary during the whole process. Fortune emphasizes this need in her list of cautions for clergy helping abused people or survivors:

Do not minimize the incidents that a victim shares with you. Assume that you are only being shown the tip of the iceberg.

Do not try to deal with the problem alone. You probably don't have the time, energy or expertise that you need. *Refer. Refer. Refer.*[6] [emphasis in original]

The helper needs to have some knowledge of local

specialized resources and counsellors. He can help the survivor decide on the right time to go into counselling, using Walsh and Liddy's guidance:

> Counselling is a slow journey, taking anything from six months to a year, sometimes even longer. As well as time it takes courage and patience. It is a painful experience because there is so much hurt around sexual abuse . . . You will not fall apart, but you will feel fragile for a time . . . Other people and areas of your life may have to be put on hold for a while as you concentrate on yourself.[7]

The pain of returning memory

Referring on does not mean abandoning the survivor to an expert. She will need people to walk with her during her journey. It is useful for helpers and friends to understand something of the process of remembering and dealing with sexual abuse in childhood. If the memory has been repressed, remembering often brings a sense of relief which feels like resolution – but not for long. Hansen discovered:

■ Buried with my memory were all the violent feelings associated with it, which I had never allowed myself to feel. There were anger, terror, hatred, grief, shame, bitterness, rage and searing emotional pain. These sprang up into the present with all the freshness and spontaneity of a child's feelings. They totally overwhelmed me and made it impossible for me to sleep, eat or work. I was submerged in what I would later realise was delayed rape trauma.[8]

Dorothy dealt with the trauma of her niece's rape by her father, still without remembering that she herself had been abused by him as a little girl. Her body remembered before her mind – physical and psychosomatic illness were the precursor to memory, and it was a long process:

■ After the incident with my niece, I still didn't remember, but I became very ill emotionally. I was convinced I had AIDS

71

and was going to die. I insisted on having a test for it, and when it came back negative I was sure it was wrong, and wanted it done again. It was totally irrational, and my rational mind was telling me it was irrational, but it was no good. When I went to church, I wouldn't go to communion in case anyone caught AIDS from me. Fortunately for me, my GP was interested in psychology and began to understand what was going on with me. He referred me for psychotherapy. If he'd put me on tranquillizers I don't know what would have become of me.

I find with my own story that I can never tell it all, it's too enormous. The enormity of it overwhelms me. So I can only tell little bits at a time.

The pain of the memory is often worsened by a sense of confusion surrounding it. Hansen, raped as a child by a trusted family friend, wondered if her terrible memories were just a nightmare:

■ Because I had been very young then, I had no sexual knowledge or vocabulary, and because I had shut the memory out so firmly, my later understanding had not been allowed to interpret the terrible thing that had happened to me. So I was very unclear, initially, on what exactly I felt the need to tell.[9]

Any Christian, lay or clergy, may be in the position of wanting to help someone who is beginning to deal with memories of child sexual abuse. The survivor's distress can be frightening; the helper may feel helpless and hopeless. In fact the helper has an important part to play just by being there for the survivor, listening to him, staying with him, affirming him, supporting him in finding any specialist help he needs.

Colin Carr, a Dominican prior who has counselled several abuse survivors, says, 'They taught me about abuse. I knew nothing about it, and nothing in my training prepared me for what they told me, except the fact that I was trained to be a good listener. I listened, and they told me.'

It is important for the helper to affirm the survivor's feelings, as she may be doubting her own memory and sanity. The helper may express her own feelings also; her anger at the abuse may free the survivor to be angry on her own behalf, and this is one of the steps she needs to take towards resolution.

Grief

The grief of abused people goes on and on. The mourning for the destruction of a child knows no bounds. We need not be frightened by or keep our distance from this grief; it is entirely appropriate. The Christian tradition offers resources to mediate grief; Hansen drew on the Old Testament to help express her own:

> Sorrow overtakes me,
> my heart fails me.
> Listen, the cry of the daughter of my people
> sounds throughout the land . . .
> The wound of the daughter of my people
> wounds me too. (Jeremiah 8.18)[10]

Trible pointed out for the first time how the Old Testament noted the pain of abused women and children, even where there was no recognition or recompense within their society at the time.[11] In her chapter 'On telling sad stories' she points out that, contrary to many moral tales, justice is not done in the end, the innocent are not vindicated. 'To seek the redemption of these stories in the resurrection is perverse. Sad stories do not have happy endings.' She quotes the story of Tamar, King David's daughter, raped by her older brother Amnon:

> Tamar took ashes upon her head
> And the long robe that was on her she tore.
> She put her hand upon her head
> And she went out; and as she went, she wept . . .
> So Tamar dwelt, and she was desolate,
> In the house of Absalom her brother.

Margaret Kennedy has written a moving lament for an abused child: a set of Stations of the Cross, which is – as the Stations should be – a long cry of grief and horror. She brings together the experience of the child and the survivor, travelling back in time during the Stations. The journey towards the

Cross – the betrayal, sneers, desolation, falls (into suicide attempts) – expresses the survivor's *Via Dolorosa*, but on approaching the Cross the child victim appears, stripped of her garments, deserted and inwardly dying:

> Your father locked the door and closed the windows. He put a pillow over your face so that no one heard your screams. You were well and truly nailed to your cross . . . He was a big man. His body became the nails. He pinned you so tight against him you could not get away.[12]

Bass and Davis emphasize the importance of grieving:

> You may feel foolish crying over events that happened so long ago. But grief waits for expression. When you do not allow yourself to honor grief, it festers. It can limit your vitality, make you sick, decrease your capacity for love.
>
> Grief has its own rhythms. You can't say, 'Okay, I'm going to grieve now.' Rather you must allow room for those feelings when they arise. Grief needs space. You can only really grieve when you give yourself the time, security, and permission to grieve.[13]

The rush to resurrection

This is a particular problem in Christianity. Because we believe in the healing power of Christ's resurrection, we may expect Christianity to heal all grief speedily. This seems to be more characteristic of the evangelical wing of the church than of others, but it can be found anywhere, because it arises mostly out of our fear of evil and pain, and our anxiety to find some kind of spiritual band-aid. It is also a very mechanistic view, assuming a facility in healing which denies the depth of the damage done. How can the survivor be convinced that God accepts and loves him, if God's Church distances itself from him and refuses to understand the reality of his pain?

Anger

The angriest words in the gospel are Jesus' tirade against those who harm children: they would be better off thrown into the depths of the sea with a millstone tied round their necks. Yet Christianity often seems to label anger as sinful. Hansen resisted her own anger until given permission to express it:

■ There was anger, fury might be a better word, hatred, grief, bitterness, resentment . . . I felt guilty about all these feelings – anger and hatred are not Christian . . . It is hard to feel sorry for anger that feels so fully justified, or think about forgiveness for a crime against a small child, the effects of which have spread through a lifetime.[14]

Anger may be the key to change, both personal and communal. Campbell relates anger to justice-making:

The greatest ally of injustice is political apathy, a mentality which leaves in the hands of 'experts' the fate of our fellow-humans. When the gospel comes alive in the place where the despised and rejected are to be found, we see with open eyes what we permit to happen in our name, and in the unsettling experience of anger at oppression we may find the words which are ours to speak, the questions we must ask and the humility to hear for the first time the cry of the oppressed.[15]

Survivors may be angry with God, for allowing defenceless children to be abused. Even those who have given up their religion may be left with a residue of fury that is not allowed to be expressed. Imbens and Jonker, Christian therapists working in Holland, encouraged their interviewees to write what they wanted to say to God:

■ God is the Father in Heaven who does everything for his children because he loves them . . .
God gave me a mother who didn't want me. She always told me I ruined her life.
God gave me a father who raped and abused me for 30 years.

God gave me a husband who constantly abused me and my children.
God gave my little girl a father who wanted to rape her when she was three and a half.
Well thank you very much God, that you wanted to give me all this and that you loved me so much. But God, I need nothing more from you, do you hear me? I want absolutely nothing from you; just leave me alone, please.
Let me live my own life, goddammit . . .[16]

This kind of anger may be shocking to Christians who may want to exempt God from the abused person's wrath. But we have no right to veto her anger. Why does God allow such evil? The survivor who expresses her rage and grief may later come to feel, as one of the Dutch survivors did, that God is in solidarity with her suffering, on her side, abused like her. Some survivors whose abuse took place in an oppressively religious context may need to leave the church for a time. Some never return, particularly those who see the church as not only rejecting them but welcoming and elevating their abusers:

■   Angry as I was, I continued to attend church . . . Yet I was aware of a growing sense of uncomfortableness. I was attending the same church the perpetrator of my childhood abuse was attending. In addition, a former pastor who had displayed inappropriate sexual behavior towards me when I earlier asked for help also attended the same church. And finally, the man who raped me was called into service by the larger church and cited for his contributions to the church. My body ached with the inconsistency of behavior in their lives. I soon recognized I was being victimized by the church again. After three years of internal struggle I slowly withdrew from the church. It was just this past spring that I finally left. It was difficult to leave a church after forty-six years.[17]

[The survivor] turns her back on religion and the church . . . Priests . . . can react very nonchalantly: 'If she's not happy with us, she's better off leaving.' But to whom does the church belong, then? Is it not *her* church too? . . . The criminals remain members, while the survivors, who have also been wounded in their souls, flee the church.[18]

Some survivors lose their faith and never recover it.

■ After [the abuse started], God became untrustworthy and Jesus was like someone out of a fairytale. That's when everything came crashing in on me. It's becoming increasingly clear to me that incest is the main thing responsible for destroying my faith.[19]

Anger is a necessary stage in the process of mourning and healing. It is right for the survivor to stop blaming himself and become angry. Some may recover their faith and come back to their church. Whether or not they do the church should recognize the validity of their anger and support them in expressing it and moving on.

Suffering

Some Christian children are brought up in religious traditions which emphasize and honour suffering. Catholic children used to be told to 'offer it up' in atonement for their own sins or the sins of others. Suffering willingly accepted is seen as a path to salvation.

This may become an obstacle to recovery for the abused person. If suffering meekly borne is a source of grace, what is the point of trying to escape from it? If God is just, surely the suffering inflicted must be deserved in some way? The American theologians comment on the problematic point that God, in sending his son to die, could be seen as an abusive father:

The image of God the Father demanding and carrying out the suffering and death of his own son has sustained a culture of abuse and led to the abandonment of victims of abuse and oppression. Until this image is shattered it will be almost impossible to create a just society.[20]

Brown and Bohn criticize the idea that good can come out of suffering, and reject all attempts to justify it.[21]

Survivors who have worked through their abuse, especially those who have found the support and understanding they need, make the point that although abuse is always bad, those who suffer it may grow in wisdom and maturity. Hansen found that:

■ These years of working through the trauma have been the most valuable of my life, through them I have learned that the new life promised by the Gospel is a reality made accessible to us. The Gospel is for desperate people.[22]

Whatever their understanding of it, the issue of suffering will always arise for abused people who are Christians. Their helpers need to address it sensitively and intelligently, and resist the temptation to fall back on easy answers.

Guilt

This is not just a religious issue; most survivors have taken on the shame and guilt of what was done to them. For Christians, however, who are taught from childhood about the Fall and the universal sinfulness of the human race, it is more insidious. They have been brought up to accept that sinfulness is inescapable, and may find it hard to realize their innocence of the abuse inflicted on them. The residue of guilt and shame derives from their childhood understanding of what happened. If the child could not escape, or felt he must obey his abuser, this degree of compliance may be experienced as shared guilt for the abuse. If the abuser implied that the child had an element of choice, consent or enjoyment, and repeats it often enough, the child begins to believe it. The adult survivor is left with the nagging questions:

- Why didn't I stop it?
- Why didn't I tell someone?
- What did I do that made her abuse me?
- What is it about me that made me a target?

These questions must be elucidated, or they will go on

undermining the abused person's struggle towards survival. Pastoral helpers must not just dismiss these questions; they should educate themselves to understand where the questions come from, why they are still so tormenting, and how they can be resolved.

Forgiveness

■ The issue of forgiveness is a very difficult one, especially for someone who has excused, denied and attempted to forgive all her life and has only recently begun to learn about anger and hatred. The only God I can believe in is one who accepts honest emotions and healthy responses. (Dorothy, a Tyneside abuse survivor)

Forgiveness is often seen as part of the healing process: healing of the abused person, in that it is supposed to help to free him from the past, and of the abuser, since it is supposed to help him to repent and change his ways.

In some cases, forgiveness of the abuser is experienced as liberating:

■ I must tell you that I have been able to forgive the woman who abused me. This is all part of the healing process. There must be forgiveness. I now have a really good relationship with her.

She became a Christian about two years after me, and she can't remember any of the past bad times with me. I'm really glad she can't![23]

In such a case, niggling anxieties may remain. Conversion seems to mean amnesia, for the abuser. Does she still have access to children, and if so, how is their safety assured?

We have already seen examples of abused people being urged to forgive their abusers. One survivor comments, 'I think a lot of Christians find it easiest to say, "If this person had enough faith, she could forgive her abuser and forget." '

A minister asked me recently in a discussion group, 'Suppose my father had abused my children, and later asks me to forgive him – I should, shouldn't I? I should seek to restore the relationship, let him be a grandad to them again, let him spend time with them?' I asked him to consider in practical terms what was meant by restoring the relationship. Would he and his abusing father honestly believe it was now safe for the abuser to have free access to the children again? If they did, had his father honestly admitted the reality of his offending behaviour, and the hold it had over him? How did the children feel about it? Were their safety, physical, mental and moral integrity to be gambled on unrealistic expectations?

In such a case, real forgiveness should be rooted in reality. The father might say something like, 'I want to forgive you, and therefore I will help you to accept the reality of your situation. I will not put you at risk of hurting your grand-children again by recklessly exposing you to a temptation which you know in your heart of hearts you cannot resist. If they freely choose to see you from time to time, I will arrange safe access for you to visit them with one of their parents present. I will grieve with you for the loss of the relationship you could have had with children, and help you come to terms with the more limited but safe relationship you can have. I will help you to seek out therapy to deal with your behaviour towards children.' (Of course this is an oversimplification. If the grandfather has abused his own grandchildren, he may well have abused his own child – the father or mother – and there will be these feelings to deal with as well.)

Let us consider the more facile view of forgiveness, imposed as a Christian duty without considering its implications. The abused person may well be exhorted by a pastor to forgive the abuser, on the grounds that Christ said we must forgive seventy times seven times. If she feels unable to forgive, this demand may feel like a bullying misuse of authority which mirrors her childhood abuse. The Church may unwittingly be colluding with the abuser, who has manipulated the victim's feelings in childhood and can now readily produce tears and expressions of regret in order to be let off the hook. If he achieves this easily, he will normally co-opt such ready for-giveness as tacit permission to carry on abusing. The abused person may be saying, in effect, 'You hurt me dreadfully, and that pain is still with me, but I forgive you. I set you free unconditionally; your future behaviour is between you and God.' To the abuser who has enjoyed his power over his victim, the knowledge of her pain may be a secret source of gratification. At the same time, her forgiveness may be interpreted by him as permission to continue abusing. The survivor cannot carry the responsibility for her abuser's future victims, but those who exhort her to forgive should have some thought for them.

Reluctance or slowness to forgive, therefore, is not a falling short of a Christian ideal; it is rooted in the reality of sin and the meaning of forgiveness. The abuser can achieve forgiveness, both from the church and from his victim, but this must be in response to real repentance (not just feelings of remorse), including a resolution never to hurt children again. Pellauer puts this into a theologica context:

> Sometimes . . . an abusive father confesses, asks forgiveness and promises never to sexually approach his daughter again . . . The minister/rabbi is then put in a position of assuring forgiveness and evaluating the strength of the person's promise not to abuse again. While the abuser may be genuinely contrite, he or she is seldom able to end the abuse without assistance and treatment.
>
> The minister/rabbi needs to assure the person of God's forgiveness and must confront the person with the fact that he or she needs additional help in order to stop the abuse.[24]

Pellauer makes the point that the issue of forgiveness is not entirely separate from the issue of justice, of putting things right. If there is no will, on the part of the church, society or the abuser, to put things right, forgiveness looks farcical:

> . . . often forgiveness is interpreted to mean to forget or pretend the abuse never happened. Neither is possible. The abuse will never be forgotten; it becomes a part of the victim's history. Forgiveness is a matter of the victim's being able to say that she will no longer allow the experience to dominate her or his life – and will let go of it and move on. This is usually possible if there is some

sense of justice in the situation, officially (through the legal system) or unofficially. Forgiveness by the victim is possible when there is repentence on the part of the abuser, and real repentence means a change in the abuser's behaviour.[25]

Having set forth this ideal, it must be remembered that this amount of progress is not achieved in most cases of child sexual abuse. The norm, for most abused people, is to live with the tormenting knowledge that their abusers have got off scotfree, ridicule their former victims, and are still abusing children. It is common for abusers to maintain an abusive hold on former victims. If the survivor does denounce her abuser, he will usually respond by smearing her, calling her mad and vicious. The gentle minister's wife whom I quoted earlier in this chapter was ostracized by her family when she spoke about her abuse (mainly for the sake of other children in the family to whom her grandfather had access). The most badly hurt woman I know ('Sally' in chapter 1) is still very much in the power of the parents who abused her sexually, physically and emotionally in her childhood. They track her down when-ever she moves house, and visit periodically to cajole, threaten and terrorize her. They accuse her of being unhinged, and have made her so emotionally fragile that this may become a self-fulfilling prophecy, if she does not retreat into suicide, which she holds onto as an escape route. Forgiveness in this case would mean nothing, and would certainly not free her from them.

If forgiveness involves justice-making and awareness of how an abuser endangers all the children in his community, the church's role in mediating it must be very carefully thought out. It may begin with something that looks like the opposite of forgiveness – confrontation and denunciation.

These are not always seen as part of pastoral duty. Yet a firm confrontation fulfils two functions. It can be the first step towards forgiveness for the abuser and recovery for the victim. The pastoral value of confrontation was shown by a woman deacon, who was counselling an abuse survivor (Elizabeth, in chapter 1). When Elizabeth decided to confront her family with her father's abuse, he swore, 'Before God, I have never had sex with anyone but my wife.' The deacon replied, 'Before God, you have!' For once, the church's strong words of authority were spoken on behalf of the victim.

Confrontation is not always possible or wise, and only the survivor can tell if she feels ready and safe to do it. The dangers are real. Some abusers get sexual satisfaction from understanding how much they have hurt their victims, and how long the pain has lasted. They see the sad and bitter accusations as an acknowledgement of their power. The survivor's reluctance to confront her abuser is prudent and realistic. But where she is ready and feels able to do it, the support of her minister can help her to carry out her task safely, and help the abuser to accept the reality of what he has done.

Marie Fortune, founder of the Center for the Prevention of Sexual and Domestic Violence (Seattle), warns clergy against 'cheap grace' – easy forgiveness and premature reconciliation, without rebuke or repentance. She calls it, after Jeremiah, 'healing the wound of my people lightly, saying Peace, peace, when there is no peace.' She describes the work of restitution that must be carried out before forgiveness is possible, and stresses that it must not be seen as a way of avoiding the criminal justice system or the statutory child-protection system:

> It is important that the criminal justice system be used if at all possible, because it unequivocally communicates that the offender is held accountable for the abuse and it has the best chance of directing the offender to treatment . . .
>
> Withholding forgiveness and absolution from an offender until certain conditions have been met may be the best way to facilitate a permanent change.[26]

Religious issues and spirituality

Abuse survivors who are Christians have to deal with a range of religious issues which non-Christians may be inclined to dismiss: the meaning of suffering, forgiveness, the sanctity of the family, obedience to parents, relating to God as father.

Constructive engagement with these issues can help the survivor to seek out and be nurtured by what is good and true within her faith tradition, while identifying what is inessential or unhelpful. The fatherhood of God, for instance, while insisted upon as central in some traditions, is only an image and need not be used if it is a stumbling block to the survivor. Forgiveness and suffering need scrutiny and analysis. These issues need to be taken seriously, for they are very real to the survivor.

The question arises: are Christian or secular sources of help more effective for Christian survivors? Does Christianity, as some evangelicals would suggest, offer a universally better route to healing than secular resources? Or does it do more harm than good, as some survivors who have been abused or damaged by the Church might suggest?

There has been a great divorce between Church and secular agencies on this question, each excluding the other's potential for healing. Kennedy deplores this situation, but explains the reasons for it:

> Therapists are typically prepared, by disposition and training, to view all but the most watered-down religion as pathogenic . . . mental health workers in general and psychodynamic psychotherapists in particular have traditionally isolated the patient's religious beliefs system from the healing process of psychotherapy. For many professionals religion is seen as a dependency crutch . . . Some Christians view psychotherapy as almost blasphemous, as a reflection of lack of faith and the power of prayer . . . The result is that the religious adult client survivor is left with a conflictual choice between a competent therapist hostile to cherished beliefs or a like-minded parochial counsellor with less of the needed therapeutic expertise or a counsellor whose rigid understanding of sin and guilt reinforce [sic] guilt and shame.[27]

It is essential that secular and religious resources co-operate in helping abuse survivors. Religious helpers must recognize the extra dimensions of expertise and training the secular counsellor can offer; secular counsellors must recognize and respect the importance of the religious issues that arise for abuse survivors. Pellauer suggests these guidelines for the secular counsellor:

1. Pay attention to religious questions/comments/references.

2. Affirm these concerns as appropriate and check out their importance for the client.

3. Having identified and affirmed this area of concern, if you are uncomfortable with it yourself or feel unqualified to pursue it, refer to a pastor/priest/rabbi who is trained to help and whom you know and trust.

4. If you are comfortable and would like to pursue the concern, do so, emphasizing the ways in which the client's religious tradition can be a resource to her or him and can in no way be used to justify or allow abuse or violence to continue in the family.[28]

Marie Fortune calls the Church to a faithful response to victims of abuse or domestic violence:

Many women turn to their faith traditions when they face the crisis of sexual or domestic violence. They deserve to find a faithful response so that they need not abandon their faith in order to stop their victimization.
. . . Spirituality is the last 'closet' of the women's movement. Because traditional institutions and faith practices have done so much harm to so many women, some feminist organizations reject any semblance of religious or spiritual activity. Many women, however, have retained those aspects of their faith that have nurtured and supported them, and some are now willing to speak openly of such things.
. . . We must affirm spirituality in its pluralism of expression. We cannot and should not allow this to be taken from us nor our access to it denied.[29]

Spirituality is not confined to churches, and several Christian survivors have commented that they found help from secular counsellors who acknowledged their clients' spirituality and spoke of their own. Bass and Davis describe the importance of spirituality in healing:

> A healing spirituality is . . . a passion for life, a feeling of connection, of being part of the life around you. Many people experience this in nature, watching the ocean roll in, looking over a vast prairie, walking in the desert. When you are truly intimate with another human being, when you are uplifted through singing, when you look at a child and feel wonder, you are in touch with something bigger than yourself . . . There's a part of everything living that wants to become itself – the tadpole into the frog, the chrysalis into the butterfly, a damaged human being into a whole one. And that's spirituality: staying in touch with the part of you that is choosing to heal, that wants to be healthy, integrated, fully alive. The little part of you that is already whole can lead the rest of you through the healing process.[30]

Matthew Fox calls this 'panentheism': the experience of transcendence felt in the beauty of the natural world. It is important to many survivors, perhaps because they cannot trust humans. Dorothy, abused and rejected by her family (see chapter 1), speaks of being nurtured by the Northumberland hill-country:

■ When I was little no one mothered me or cuddled me, but I used to stay with relatives on a farm, and I would go walking among the round green border hills. I felt as if those breast-shaped hills were mothering me, and the earth warmed me. When I was little I would lie on the ground and cuddle into the earth and listen to the trees. I got my mothering from the landscape then, and I do now, and that's where I feel closest to God. There, I have no doubts about my faith. I feel held, but not healed. Something is holding onto me while I am going through the pain, but it doesn't lessen it or shorten it.

Rites of passage

The abused person's journey from victimization to survival

should be supported and celebrated by his faith community. Several beautiful liturgies are available for this; Pellauer has collected some of them in a chapter of 'Litanies, psalms and songs'. Hansen's liturgy of healing could be used by individuals or adapted for use by groups. Kennedy's Stations of the Cross have already been quoted. Most of these prayers and liturgies have been produced by and for abuse survivors. Kennedy, who has helped the Roman Catholic community in Britain to understand the problem of csa, feels that her church does not make sufficient use of the ministry of survivors:

> There should be prayers, liturgies, healing services for abused people. The need is desperate. Our group [a Christian survivors' group in London] is here as a resource, yet I am not even allowed to put up our notices in churches. We are ready and willing to help, but some people don't want to hear.

5

The war against children

I have discussed individual cases of abuse, but child sexual abuse is not a collection of separate aberrations. The statistics show that it is a widespread social problem. Society in various ways allows it and condones it, and the churches, to the extent that they do not speak out against it, collude with it. Child abuse and societal refusal to deal with it amount to a systematic onslaught on children, who are powerless to defend themselves. The churches should be ready to defend children; to do so they need information and discernment. In particular they need to understand the links between individual cases of abuse and the wider social processes which fail children.

Discerning good and evil

Examples have already been given of the tendency, even among Christians, to imply that csa is not a grave matter. I have heard Christians muddy the waters by suggesting a kind of moral neutrality; an eminent priest I met at a recent conference persistently asked whether sexual abuse was not common practice in some 'primitive African tribes'. This is one of a range of myths, a system of cognitive distortions which effectively camouflage good and evil and obstruct a clear analysis.

In such an atmosphere of confusion and sometimes deliberate obfuscation, simple truths can get lost. The embarrassing and unmanageable five-year-old boy who wants to bugger the other children at his infants' school may be the object of pity and regret, but is also commonly seen as a distasteful, nasty little boy, not as what he is – an innocent child of God who has been dreadfully wronged. The survivor beset by despair and self-hatred, perhaps grumpy and wearisome as she struggles to save her spirit from disintegration, may be seen as an antisocial personality rather than a heroine. Both these people, adult and child, need commitment and solidarity from their community if they are to survive their ordeal.

Smokescreens and looking-glass worlds

Victims feel guilty; abusers present themselves as victims. Evil is presented as its opposite. These distortions may have wormed their way into our consciousness so effectively that we do not discern them. A good exercise is to look critically at the assertions made by abusers in reported cases, and examine our own reaction to them:

- 'The child was a flirt. She led me on.' (This is a common accusation. In one case a grandfather accused his grand-daughter of being 'provocative'. She was eighteen months old. She had lain with her legs apart when he changed her nappy.)

- 'Her mother knew about it. She encouraged me to teach the girl about sex. It was all her fault.'

- 'He did not say anything so I assumed he was enjoying it.'

- 'Abuse doesn't do much harm – it's society's reaction which traumatizes the child.'

- 'Intervention to stop the abuse is worse than the abuse itself.'

The abuser's cognitive distortions disguise the abuse and shift responsibility from where it belongs. The victim lives in a looking-glass world, where her abuser tells her she is to blame and society seems to believe the same. Abusers do not have to work very hard at creating a safe environment for abuse; the mythology they create finds ready acceptance.

For example, adults will ostensibly agree that children should be free from oppression and abuse, but they interpret this in various ways. In the 'sexual revolution' of the 1960s, this principle was interpreted vigorously and publicly by the then legal Paedophile Information Exchange (PIE) as children's freedom to be abused, or (in their language) to 'express and develop their own sexuality' with adult partners. We can see the absurdity of this view now (though it is still doubtless held by many abusers), but at the time many liberal-thinking people were tempted to believe it.

Such myths amount to a propaganda war waged by abusers against children, a war in which Christians have a duty to take sides. There are attitudes hostile to children current now, and pressure groups currently regarded as reputable, that will be seen by future generations as questionable. PIE is now illegal, and its old files provide dated but still useful evidence for the police to investigate networks of child-molesters.

Other organizations may also, whether wittingly or un-wittingly, impede efforts to tackle csa. VOCAL (Victims of Child Abuse Laws) is an organization set up in the USA in the mid-1980s with the declared aim of defending parents against 'over-zealous social workers' and protecting the rights of defendants. Perhaps their most powerful activity is to create networks among people dedicated to contesting allegations of abuse. A VOCAL newsletter carried an advertisement by a group called Men International, who boast that their 'A-team' ('A' for 'annihilation') can smash such allegations.[1]

An inescapable problem for such an organization is that, even if its founders do not include abusers seeking protection and support, it will inevitably act as a magnet for them.

Indeed, VOCAL have been forced to acknowledge that they number abusers among their members.[2]

In the UK, PAIN (Parents Against Injustice) provided evidence to the Butler-Sloss enquiry in Cleveland in 1987, criticizing child care professionals for raising the concern of csa. Is this really in the best interests of children?

In October 1992, PAIN announced a report of a 'case study of thirty families who claim to have been falsely accused'.[3] This terminology is nonsensical and disturbing in itself. A diagnosis or concern of child sexual abuse is not an 'accusation' of an individual and certainly not of a family. PAIN recommend their report to 'all who believe in the well-being of children and the preservation of family life'. In the context of intra-familial abuse, these two ideals cannot always go hand in hand. They may need to be reconciled in the context of a family made safe for the child by the exclusion of an abuser. The family should not be an idol to which the child is sacrificed if it contains an abuser.

Guilt and responsibility

In a world, then, where child abuse can masquerade as 'children's lib' and adult supremacism masquerades as civil liberty, it is particularly important to have a clear idea of the evil involved in csa, and the responsibility of its perpetrators.

Mary Midgley[4] and Michael Bavidge[5] have commented on the current conflict between two views of evil, one which attributes evildoing to individual character and personality, and one which blames exterior, social conditions and pressures. Both are deterministic and tend to erode the element of individual choice and control. The 'social conditions' view has held sway in this century, as a reaction against the more religious, earlier view of personal wickedness. In fact this is an overreaction, suggesting a false antithesis. Both external conditions and interior character may predispose towards evildoing, but sane people still have autonomy in choosing to do evil or good.

However, the revolt against morality has resulted, as Midgley points out, in a certain tentativeness: '. . . we fear to identify wrongdoing at all; we shrink from judging morally. Such judgement strikes us as presumptuous and self right-eous.'[6] We are accustomed, rightly, to considering the external pressures or deprivations that may predispose to crime; this should not, but sometimes does, detract from our realization of the magnitude of the harm done.

Actually, both attitudes – accusatory and excusing – are common where child abuse is concerned, and both have a common focus: the abusing adult. He is seen as a depraved beast at one moment, a victim of circumstances the next. If instead we look at the abused child, and the harm done to him or her, we are led back to considering the abuser in a far more practical way, with questions such as: 'How is the child to be healed?' 'Can the abuser atone in any way for this harm?' 'Can trust be restored?' (if it was a relationship of trust that was violated) and 'How can this adult be prevented from hurting more children?' The answers have deep implications: they demand that the adult realizes the enormity of the harm, and repents of it. The first step towards such a change of heart is to accept responsibility for the abuse.

The issue can be further evaded by averring that people who molest children must be mentally ill or abnormal in some way: 'I couldn't imagine doing anything like that, I don't believe any normal person would.' There is no basis for this assumption, but it may be an unconscious distancing reaction from such a disturbing subject. Men in particular hasten to disown this apparent psychopathology of male sexuality.

This reaction is also part of a wider assumption, the circular argument that some actions are so wicked that no sane person could carry them out, therefore anyone who commits them must be insane or subhuman; 'beast' is the commonest name for a convicted sex offender.

> It is interesting to observe how in their search for the superlatives of condemnation, headline writers describe the criminal in non-human terms. They draw on the sub- and the superhuman for revealing analogies. The criminal is a beast or a demon. He has dropped out of human society into the animal world, or he has been possessed by an alien force of superhuman malignity.[7]

This is not true. Child-molesters are men and women like the rest of us.

'He doesn't know how to love children'

They do, however, see the world from a distorted perspective. Most paedophiles have their attention increasingly concentrated on one thing. Nabokov brilliantly portrays in *Lolita* the paedophile whose whole life and intelligence is dedicated to the rape of a pre-pubertal virgin child; he woos her mother in order to gain access to the girl, and fills pages with his self-justificatory excuses. Nabokov's portrayal is so effective that some people have condemned it as a justification of child abuse, while some paedophiles take it as a serious paedophile statement, failing to discern the self-deception of the narrator and the powerlessness of the child.

As usual, it is abuse survivors who have the clearest perception of abusers:

■ When I was being abused, I just hoped it would end, and that everything would be all right, that my father would go back to being a nice daddy, and that he would love me. Now that I'm older, I realize that's impossible. He's a child-molester and he doesn't know how to love children. I don't know if there is any help for him.

Social evil

Society's oppression of children is composed of two elements: failure to act protectively to prevent harm to them, and active discrimination against them.

Having identified the individual responsibility of the abuser, it is necessary to look at the ways in which society colludes with or fails to prevent child abuse, for whatever reason (and not least, it must be assumed, because some of our law-makers and enforcers, clergy and other influential people in society, are themselves abusers).

The law

The English legal system is hallowed by age and custom; its cherished adversarial system has been developed to protect and assert the rights of each protagonist in the legal process. This system makes assumptions of neutrality and equality of opportunity which are untrue and oppressive, in the case of children.

The legal system is central to child protection, because in many cases legal sanction is the only sure defence for a child against her abuser (some mothers do protect their children in defiance of the law, but they may suffer terrible penalties for doing so; Dr Elizabeth Morgan was jailed for two years in the USA for protecting her daughter from her abusive ex-husband).

All are supposedly equal in the eyes of the law. This equality is often acknowledged to be flawed by economic disadvantage, but there are much greater flaws deriving from the structural power differential between adults and children. Of the few cases of child sexual abuse that come to light, only a fraction are prosecuted, because it is recognized that the prosecution may redouble the stress and suffering of the child. The adversarial system demands that the defence counsel harass and pressurize the child, and that the accused person, if guilty, reproduce in court the ridicule, slander and veiled threats used against the child. Many prosecutions have had to be halted because abused children became too distressed to give evidence.

Many more prosecutions are never brought at all because they would rest mainly on the child's evidence, and children cannot give sworn evidence in English courts. Yet there is no evidence that children are less truthful witnesses than adults. There would be an outcry if, say, the law did not allow black people to give evidence of criminal attacks inflicted on them; but the cruel discrimination against children goes without comment. As a result, an abuser who has molested many children can go free because the children are not allowed to corroborate each other's evidence.

The judicial process has thus become part of the abusive system. This is not a partial view; it was recognized in 1989 by the Pigot Committee, which made various recommendations concerning children's evidence: that it should where appropriate be collected in non-traditional ways, such as on video, and that cross-examination should be carried out in a humane way likely to enhance understanding, for instance in the presence of the mother or a trusted adult helper.[8] These recommendations were vigorously contested by legal bodies as encroaching on the rights of defendants, and the government rejected most of the Pigot recommendations.

What was happening in this debate? A reasonable set of principles, the traditional rights of the defendant in English law, were being asserted as an over-arching absolute good which must prevail over claims seen as marginal or contingent, for instance that the law should be just to children. What makes lawyers think that the rights of adults are automatically more important than the rights and welfare of children? Surely a humane and civilized legal system would reverse these priorities, or at least try to balance them more justly? Lawyers are bound by tradition but may consent to innovation in the law once it is seen to be right and necessary. The law in this case was made by adults, for adults, against children.

In addressing legal issues (or religious or social ones) it is important to hold on to a sense of right and wrong. The law discriminates against abused children, and that is wrong. Lawyers have not combined to change this discrimination, and that is wrong. Encroaching on the rights of defendants is not wrong, if those rights are oppressive of the rights of children. Rights are continually being balanced. One person's rights are often in conflict with those of another. A civilized society scrutinizes and monitors this balance to maintain it as justly as possible.

A confusion often arises in the area of overlap between criminal and child-care legal proceedings. An accused person should be convicted only if his guilt is established 'beyond reasonable doubt'. However, stopping a child's abuse should not have to depend on such a standard of proof. You do not wait to be sure beyond reasonable doubt that your child has meningitis before taking him to hospital. Child protection has to depend on the balance of probability. If there is good evidence that a child has been sexually abused, protective action must be taken. If a probable abuser is known – for instance, she names a relative who cannot be prosecuted on her unsworn evidence – she and other children must be protected from him. A balance must be found between the abuser's rights in the absence of a prosecution, and the child's rights. What are the rights of the community when an abuser is legally at large? What steps could be taken to protect children without stigmatizing or discriminating against him? These ethical questions cannot be resolved within a professional framework; they must be addressed by the wider community, and the churches have a crucial contribution to make to the discussion.

Power games

Child sexual abuse is an abuse of adult power. The abuser builds up his power both over his victim/s and over his immediate circle, intimidating anyone who might help the child. The non-abusing carer, if there is one, is subtly bullied, ridiculed and undermined, so that her power to help the child is lessened.

A paediatrician told me of a recent consultation where she was seeing a baby girl, brought in by her parents. At the end of the consultation the father said that the baby's nappy needed changing (though it was only slightly damp), and proceeded to change it. He took out a jar of cream and began to apply it liberally to the baby's bottom and genitals, for an unnecessarily long time. At last his wife timidly intervened to suggest that that was enough cream. He turned and snapped at her, 'Don't you *dare* tell me how to change my baby's nappy!' Then he smiled at the doctor and said, 'But I don't hit her!' (meaning his wife).

This man was not being furtive about his treatment of the baby; he was demonstrating boldly to the baby's mother and doctor that he controlled his family and did as he pleased with them, emphasizing it with a thinly veiled threat of violence.

Mothers are commonly taunted in this way. One mother I have met was sure her teenage daughter was being sexually abused by her husband, but the girl would not say anything. The mother expressed her worries, and her husband ridiculed and sneered at her. But every night when they went to bed, she found that her husband had put his toothbrush and the daughter's interlocked, bristles together – a silent taunt. What could she have said in a court of law that would not have sounded ridiculous? Years later her daughter reproached her for not stopping the abuse, and it took a long time for her to understand how powerless her mother had been, despite her best efforts.

When we wonder why children do not speak about abuse, or those close to them fail to protect them, it is important to have some idea of the resourceful, perverted power games developed by abusers.

Men in authority

La Fontaine suggests that men in authority sometimes have difficulty accepting the facts about csa. She describes a group of men prominent in the 1987 Cleveland crisis – MP, vicar, doctor:

> Prominent among those who threw doubt on the diagnoses [of child sexual abuse] and supported the parents' claim to innocence were men in positions of authority such as Stuart Bell, the Reverend Michael Wright and Dr Irvine, the police surgeon whose views strongly influenced the actions of the police. These three men were prime movers in encouraging resistance to the idea that sexual abuse had occurred. Stuart Bell in particular was very emotional in his appeals on behalf of the parents and in claiming that there was a general attack on the family. The story he told most often was that of a man whose wife, he alleged, had been 'brainwashed' into believing the accusation against him. The diagnosis made by Dr Marietta Higgs and the defection of his wife were somehow combined as the cause of his 'tragedy'. In this case, there was a strong presumption of the man's guilt . . . and tragedy seems hardly an appropriate word though it might have been used with justice for his daughter's situation. The point here is that Stuart Bell seems to have unquestioningly sided with the man concerned . . . It would appear that the strongest supporters of parental authority and the autonomy of family life are men and particularly men of some authority.[9]

There *was* a family in great need of support in this situation – the mother and the two children she protected from abuse, at the cost of loneliness and financial hardship. But their voices were not heard.

Adultism

We were all children once. Why are we not all passionate child advocates now? Psychotherapist Alice Miller coined the term 'adultism' in her analysis of why adults abuse children, or do nothing to protect them. According to her, adults suppress their own painful memories of childhood helplessness, fear and harsh treatment, and fail to respect and nurture children because they fear to reawaken those threatening memories. Miller believes in original goodness:

> People whose integrity has not been damaged in child-hood, who were protected, respected and treated with honesty by their parents will be – both in their youth and in adulthood – intelligent, responsive, empathic and highly sensitive. They will take pleasure in life and will not feel any need to . . . hurt others or themselves. They will not be able to do otherwise than respect and protect those weaker than themselves, including their children, because this is what they have learned from their own experience.[10]

Miller's work, the basis of 'inner child therapy' which helps many abuse survivors, is ultimately optimistic. Evil cannot be combated until it is named. In naming the evils of child abuse and adultism, the churches could begin to frame ways of overcoming them.

6

Ritual abuse

All child sexual abuse is wrong. Some Christians have focused only on ritual abuse, that is, child abuse taking place in the context of what appear to be satanic rituals. There are several reasons for this:

- They may feel that there is a very powerful manifestation of demonic power, which should be confronted by Christianity (and cannot be dealt with by secular agencies).

- They may feel that ritual abuse is particularly evil because it blasphemes the Christian religion.

- Caricatures of Christian ritual may leave abuse survivors with problems in their own religious practice as adults.

Ritual abuse may well be more terrifying and harmful than other kinds of child sexual abuse. Nevertheless all child sexual abuse is evil and harmful, and all Christians should be concerned about the whole problem, not just one small, though particularly sensational, manifestation of it.

Having said that, it is necessary to set out some basic information about ritual abuse and place it in context. The debate about it has been obscured both by Christians with their own agendas and by non-Christians seeking to deny that it happens. Both sides have muddied the waters. The subject has been researched, and Christians should approach it in a responsible and informed way.

The most pervasive myth about satanic abuse is that it is a story invented by social workers and evangelical Christians, and that no evidence for it has ever been found. In fact the evidence has been well-documented by Tate, who lists half-a-dozen cases in which a successful prosecution has been brought for ritual sexual abuse.[1] Tate's book has been repeatedly attacked by a Leeds-based satanist pressure group, but his study is carefully documented, and confirmed by people working in the field. The chairperson of the National Child Abuse Network said in a review of the book, 'From knowledge of cases not known to [Tate] . . . I am persuaded that the author's analysis of fact is significantly accurate.'[2]

The problem is not lack of evidence, but an unfortunate tendency to exclude good evidence because it is seen as so weird and fantastic that juries would not believe it. Thus it may be decided to bring a prosecution for 'ordinary' child abuse, and ignore extensive evidence of rituals. Bea Campbell, who studied the 1987 Nottingham ritual abuse cases, says this is a betrayal of children:

> These children's words present challenges to the agencies which should protect them. We must not filter, reorganise or reinterpret children's witness to fit our own interpretations. Adults do not want to base prosecutions on 'incredible' evidence – so they squander the clear evidence that the children give them.[3]

Ritual, satanic or network abuse?

In any discussion of ritual abuse, the question of definitions arises. Organized, network abuse, with communal systematic preparation and planning, and routines which both abusers and (perforce) victims adhere to, may be ritual abuse for all practical purposes. The use of trappings and procedures to

terrify the child are just as effective whether the abuser is
dressed as the Devil or Mickey Mouse. Is the abuse rightly
defined as satanic if there are devil-figures about? Does it
perhaps depend on whether the abusers believe in satanism or
are just using the accoutrements for their own ends? But the
anguish and terror of the child are real whether or not the
satanism is real, so does it make any difference? Indeed,
people with a sadistic paedophilic bent may well join satanic
cults specifically to abuse children, with no 'sincere' belief in
satanism. Do 'real' satanists conjure up more evil than cynical
play-actors? The urge for power over vulnerable children, the
desire to dominate, degrade and pervert them, is devilish
whatever the trappings.

There is a danger that if we become fascinated by the classic
evil of satanism, we somehow class other child sexual abuse as
less evil.

The trappings of abusive rituals, however, whether Satanic
or just weird, do present some questions for Christians. Where
do these strange robes and rigmaroles derive their power
from? On the whole, from religious services and the awe and
mystery surrounding them. As Campbell points out, ritual
abuse, like many church services,

> . . . involves men dressing up in frocks of various kinds,
> and this dressing up carries a range of power and mean-
> ing. In ritual abuse, the rituals and rigmaroles of terror
> are apparent to all participants, and their purpose is to
> subordinate and terrify.[4]

There are many professions in which men and women wear
uniforms of various kinds, to denote their calling and particular area of expertise. The special clothing, including church
vestments, is meant to carry certain meanings and guarantees
– of professional integrity, genuineness and safety. Abuses
occur, and although a uniform is not utterly vitiated by a
corrupt minority, the majority who wear it must be active in
preserving the integrity that it represents, and in preventing
abuses. In addition, we should not train our children to be
unquestioningly obedient to robed figures of authority. It is
important for their safety that they should have some idea of
the difference between the office and the person holding it,

and the awareness that if they sense something wrong they have a right to speak out.

Features of ritual abuse

Accounts of ritual abuse survivors commonly include the following elements:

- Ritual abuse is often intergenerational; traditions are passed down through families. Several extended families may collaborate.

- Because whole families are involved, the abusers include women.

- Child victims are systematically degraded, often tortured. They are commonly made to eat faeces and drink blood or urine. They are terrorized by threats and by seeing pet animals ritually slaughtered.

- Child victims are drawn into the hierarchy of terror at an early age. While still subject to abuse, they are made complicit in evil; for example, they are forced to torture a younger child or kill an animal, and made to believe that they are now agents of the devil.

This is the stuff of nightmare, and most people cannot stomach more than a small amount of information about ritual abuse. But if children have to suffer it, the least adults can do is face up to the reality of it.

In 1991 I heard a sensible and balanced woman, a rape counsellor, talk about the ordeal of helping a ritual abuse survivor:

■ We didn't find any experts to help us . . . we did not know what to do, we just did what seemed essential to keep her alive. We are justifiably afraid of losing support for our work, built up over the years, but we can't say 'Sorry, we don't do ritual abuse, it's too difficult.'

Dealing with ritual abuse involves confronting huge power

structures, wealthy and powerful men . . . Men who murder and torture as a hobby, who have sophisticated methods of mind control.

We have to find ways of working with women who are both victims and abusers since childhood, and have been traumatized and psychologically damaged in ways we haven't seen before.

At the same conference a ritual abuse survivor described the life of children abused in this way:

■ Ritual abuse means that your whole life is planned, days and weeks ahead. They have chosen what you will do, what you will suffer, whether you will live or die. You are made to commit murder – or at least believe you have. Your whole life is back to front. You are taught that all good things are bad and all bad things good. The only way to survive is to forget, day by day, what you have done, what has been done to you.

Professionals helping ritually abused children are vulnerable to depression, fear and burn-out. They carry, with the children, the brunt of a concerted and calculated attack designed to isolate the child and scare off the helper.

Church responses to ritual abuse

Tim Tate is a critical observer of Christian attempts to deal with ritual abuse. He praises the sincerity and courage of helpers in the evangelical tradition, such as Dianne Core of Childwatch and Maureen Davies of the Reachout Trust, but he criticizes them for sometimes wasting evidence of ritual abuse by poor documentation or unproved assertions. He also criticizes a more low-key approach found in the Church of England, quoting an Anglican expert on satanic abuse who counsels adult survivors:

■ The people who come to see me tend to be referred from other areas. I am the chairman of the Church of England's study group on exorcism and the occult, so I generally get asked to see the hard cases . . . I listen to what they have to say; usually it does comprise the same sort of details – child abuse, murder, drugs, prostitution and occasionally cannibalism.

Quite often these people will tell me the names of those they say were involved. Sometimes . . . they are the names of famous or highly respected people. A number of survivors independently gave the name of a particular MP as being involved . . .

But when I have finished counselling a victim I always tear up any notes I have made. I make a point of destroying everything which has recorded the satanic detail . . . Have I ever passed on the information I have been given? No, I have not; I do not believe that would be proper.

This attitude – sincere and gently expressed – is part of the problem. It is an old saw – but true for all that – that for evil to triumph it is only necessary for good men to do nothing.[5]

Tate's point is that the people this minister counsels may now be adult and out of the abusive situation, but it is safe to assume that their abusers are still perpetrating the same acts, on another set of children; and it is irresponsible to take no protective action.

Tate suggests a programme of ten proposals to investigate and deal with ritual abuse. It is the most coherent and comprehensive national initiative ever put forward, and anyone who reads the evidence amassed in his grim book will feel it is overdue for implementation.

Ritual and ritualistic behaviour

Ritual sexual abuse is different in degree from other child sexual abuse, but it is worth noting that elements of ritual are commonly found in child-molesting. The child is trained and conditioned to obey certain signs or words, under threat of punishment. Thus abuse may proceed without the abuser giving any specific commands, and the child will comply without apparent force being used. This enables the abuser to pretend that the child is willing, and makes the child feel complicit in his own abuse. For example, a child being called upstairs by her father to tidy her room may know perfectly well that the room is already tidy, and also know what is expected of her; she has no choice but to go.

Such rituals can even be presented to the world as normality. A paediatrician saw a seven-year-old girl whose abuse was presented in this way:

■ She described in detail, with a lot of pain and tension in her body, how her father was regularly putting cream up her vagina and her anus, using four fingers up her anus and one up her vagina. It had become a set ritual in the family that she would have a shower, come down and say to her dad that she had a sore bottom, and they would go up to her parents' room where he would put cream up the front and back. No one else was allowed upstairs at that time. It was a household where obedience was very rigidly enforced.

At the case conference their GP realized with a shock that he had 'given permission' for this abuse. The father had said the little girl sometimes got a sore bottom, was it all right to put cream on it? The GP had answered yes, without realizing how he was being implicated in the abuser's scenario.

Ritual can thus function to 'normalize' abuse, at the same time surrounding it with the barriers of family secrecy and confidentiality; or it can facilitate the perpetration of abuse in such fantastic circumstances that the secret will be kept for ever in the face of our sheer incredulity.

Paedophile rings and child murder

Whether satanist or not, paedophile sex rings have been known to the police for years. A Cleveland MP who has discussed the problem with Scotland Yard tells me that they are normally skilled and sophisticated enough to avoid criminal charges. Paedophiles, like other unpopular groups, band together for protection and mutual help. A sex ring may be a small-scale co-operative arrangement, like the group at whose hands little Mark Tildesley died in 1984,[6] or a large-scale operation which kidnaps children or picks up runaways who subsequently disappear.[7]

7

Where do we go from here?

Awareness of child sexual abuse ebbs and flows, though for part of the population – abusers, abused children, abuse survivors – it is a fact of life. The current awareness of it, and attempts by the churches to take it seriously, are to be welcomed. There are, however, some disturbing tendencies in Christian responses. The Christian emphasis on peace and reconciliation and compassion can lead to a rush to forgiveness and resurrection which is simply denial in another guise.

The churches in the USA are some years in advance of Britain in facing up to the problem of csa. Rossetti's thoughtful book *Slayer of the Soul*[1] sets out some guidelines for crisis management and longer-term planning when abuse is revealed within a parish; for provision of support for victims and their families; for clergy and lay training; for changing abusive behaviour. This information will be useful to the churches in Britain as they gradually acquire the degree of openness about csa that has been brutally thrust upon some of the churches in the USA in recent years.

When child sexual abuse is revealed in a family, the abuser commonly denies it indignantly. If denial becomes impossible he then invites sympathy and understanding for his predicament, his loneliness, his mistakes. He keeps the focus on himself; the child remains marginalized and secondary.

There is a danger that the churches may react in a similar way, especially when clergy abusers are revealed. The strategy of cover-up and denial is becoming discredited, and a new openness is emerging. Yet the main focus still seems to be on the abuser, his efforts to be a good priest, his anguish, his spiritual struggles. All this may be valid but the balance is wrong. Consideration of the children he has hurt should come before sympathy and understanding for his pain, necessary though this is. The clergy have a position of moral leadership; they have a choice whether to continue in it if they know they are damaging their most vulnerable charges. To abuse children, to go on abusing them, to decide to continue in a pastoral role with access to vulnerable children, is evil. Non-abusing clergy should not too readily close ranks to defend and forgive the abuser; it is the victims who need their solidarity.

In *Slayer of the Soul*, one chapter is written by a priest child abuser. It is a long, confessional account of his feelings, his unhappy childhood, his own abuse, his moral confusion. His victims are almost invisible, except when he questions whether they were really hurt by what he did. The moment of revelation when he can admit what has happened, is when he discovers and identifies with the concept that 'Victims become victimizers'. He then acknowledges what he has done, but launches again into a discussion of his sadness, sense of loss, alienation.

It is hurtful to abuse survivors to read Christian discussions of clergy abuse which seem to attend more to the abuser's needs than to those of the victims. Clergy who are abuse survivors and do not molest children may be alienated and angered to read accounts in which abusing clergy blame their offending behaviour on their own childhood victimization.

Placa discusses the problem of abusive clergy in a great deal of clinical detail, aiming to clarify which are 'safe' to return to ministry under certain conditions and which are not. He is motivated by concern for victims, abusers, the church's good name, and the church's assets, which should be used for good works rather than compensating the victims of abusive clergy.

He speaks from experience, but does not make an absolutely convincing case. He asks, for example:

> What is to be done with the man who, on one or two isolated occasions, has misconducted himself sexually with young children, but is not diagnosed as a fixated paedophile? What is to be done with the man who had misconducted himself sexually with young people, but is an ephebophile [oriented to adolescents] rather than a paedophile?[2]

'One or two isolated occasions' may be all that have come to light, but this is unlikely to represent the true extent of abusive behaviour; and the 'ephebophile' may have abused younger victims who have not disclosed. Perhaps parishioners, rather than the hierarchy, should have the chance to say whether they want a man who had 'misconducted himself sexually' with children to have continuing access to children. The very terminology chosen by this writer contains an element of denial. 'Misconducting oneself' sounds like little more than a slight breach of etiquette, and the action is defined as something done 'with' rather than 'to' children, as if there were some equality and consent.

Placa's suggested treatment programme for abusers, incorporating many of the ideas of the 'Sexaholics Anonymous' group, also places too much emphasis on abuse as a misuse of sexuality, whereas most authorities agree that misuse of power is a more important element.

It would not be right to assert that no paedophile should ever continue in a post where he has contact with children; but the onus is certainly on the hierarchy to prove that such people are safe if it intends to place them within reach of children again. Compassion is needed, but active compassion should be expressed first for past and future victims.

These issues remain to be resolved by the churches. It is to be hoped, in any case, that there will never be a return to the infamous 'geographical solution', which systematically presented abusers with a new home and a new set of victims as soon as any suspicion of abuse leaked out.

The first step: to do least harm

If the problem is approached from the point of view of children rather than abusers, some basic recommendations can be made at once. The churches can set an example to society in protecting children from known paedophiles, while helping the paedophile to seek treatment and a new way of life. At present there are few safeguards in place to make churches safe for children. A prison chaplain expresses a gloomy but realistic view:

■ I work with sex offenders a lot. Because I was abused myself I can see the way they work, and cut through a lot of the self-deception, try to break into their cycle of abusing. There's one fellow who's getting out next year, and I know exactly what he's going to do. He's going to target a vulnerable young mother, a single parent, and he's going to charm his way into that family, and make himself indispensable. Then he's going to start abusing the children. And he's going to find the family via a church. I've seen it many times. People from the church are already writing to him in prison.[3]

Local churches could offer care and support to sex offenders by finding church work for them which does not involve children, by being ready to talk openly about their offending and their feelings about it, by providing emergency counsellors for the offender to contact when he knows he is at risk of abusing, and by making parents aware that he is not safe with children.

Similarly, ministers and pastoral workers who abuse children should be firmly prevented from having any further contact with children until there is a reasonable certainty that they can and will control their molesting, which in many cases may not be achievable.

The next step: becoming a source of help for children, abuse survivors and non-abusing carers

Few churches can offer the specialized counselling needed by abused children and abuse survivors, but local churches could play a vital part in the healing process by offering understanding and support when csa is revealed. To be able to offer this, ministers and pastoral groups will need to use a training course developed for the churches, and compile a database of local helping agencies. The training packs produced in the USA by Marie Fortune and in the UK by Helen Armstrong of the National Children's Bureau are both excellent (see bibliography). There is no substitute for training, and it needs to be undertaken by anyone who might want to offer help.

The ministry of abuse survivors

One mistake which the churches may fall into with all good intentions is exploitation of abuse survivors in an effort to understand the problem. I have said several times that the information available about csa comes from abuse survivors; they are the experts. This does not mean that they should have to do all the teaching. Life is already enough of an ordeal for them without continually having to explain to one person after another the basis of their grief and pain. One young woman I talked to had been greatly helped by an Anglican minister, who in turn had learned a lot from her. But at times, through ignorance, the minister had offered inappropriate help or failed to understand a problem, and this had been painful for the survivor. There is an urgent need to formalize what we know and incorporate it in training, so that ministers who encounter the problem do not have to reinvent the wheel. Survivors have a right to say: 'If you still do not understand, that is your problem. Go and learn. Don't suck us dry – organize and finance some proper training, and make it an integral part of clergy formation.'

Whatever training is organized should however have an ongoing input from survivors and involve local survivors' groups in whatever ways seem appropriate. Their contribution should be formally recognized, and they should be represented on boards of social responsibility and training bodies. This is not a marginal issue.

Building the child-loving society

This book has dealt with the incidence of csa, the harm done, responses to csa and the search for healing. However well we learn to deal with it, it would be infinitely better if children were not sexually abused in the first place. Sadly, this seems a remote prospect; csa is deeply embedded in our society. Nothing less than a spiritual transformation of the world would bring it to an end. Bagley and King describe this as 'primary prevention':

> Child sexual abuse will continue as long as we simply focus on individual children, one at a time, applying crisis measures when abuse is revealed. It is also important, but not enough, that children and families and offenders are healed after sexual abuse happens. A more general healing of society is required to change attitudes which promote and condone sexually abusive behaviours.[4]

Social healing is needed both to prevent further child abuse, and to provide solidarity and support for abuse survivors:

> Throughout their lives, survivors struggle to heal from the injuries they suffer from sexual violence. Their healing includes a search for loving community that can provide an environment for support and understanding. In their search for community they uncover the complicity of social institutions and ideologies in the abuse of power.[5]

The prophetic response

What is the Church's part in building the child-loving society? The Justice and Peace movement defines the 'two feet of Christian service'. One foot, the more traditional one, is direct service: helping people in crisis. The other is working for social change: challenging the powerful people and structures that oppress people and deny their humanity. The two should be inseparable; the first without the second may simply perpetuate injustice. Helder Camara, champion of the people *sem vez e sem voz* – 'with no hope and no voice' – linked the two tasks in his celebrated comment: 'When I feed the poor they call me a saint; when I ask why the poor have no food they call me a communist.' As well as providing better services for abused children and abuse survivors, we have to ask why children are sexually abused.

There are few groups more oppressed and silenced than victims of child sexual abuse. Liberation theology has elucidated the task of liberation as the vocation of oppressed people. Abused children, however, cannot achieve their own liberation; they are dependent on the solidarity of adults to help them. The Church which is called to set the downtrodden free must attend to their plight. Child protection is everyone's responsibility. When every adult accepts that, child abuse will stop. In the words of a Chilean shanty-town mother:

> God doesn't do everything for us, but rather gives us the strength, the intelligence and the patience to work together and create a world of solidarity.[6]

Some of the information about csa is depressing. It is abuse survivors who show the possibility of restoration after devastation, a sign of hope for the future:

■ Now God has given me a second chance. He is restoring the years that the locusts have eaten. God can renew our lives. I am living testimony to that.[7]

Notes

Introduction

1. C. Poston and K. Lison, *Reclaiming Our Lives* (Boston, MA: Little, Brown and Co., 1989), p. 23.

1. 'I lost God'

1. M. Kennedy, 'Christianity – help or hindrance for the abused child or adult?' *Child Abuse Review* 5:3, Winter 1991/2, pp. 3–6.
2. J. Turner, *Home is Where the Hurt is* (Wellingborough: Thorsons, 1989), pp. 23–4.
3. ibid., p. 66.
4. *The Independent*, 14 July 1989, p. 12.
5. Granada Television, *World in Action*, 20 July 1992.
6. *Sunday Times*, 19 July 1992, p. 16.
7. L. Bennetts, 'Unholy acts', *Vanity Fair* 54:12, December 1991, pp. 130–5, 166–71.
8. ibid., p. 134.
9. *The Guardian*, 15 July 1992, p. 3.
10. *The Guardian*, 2 August 1991, p. 3.
11. *The Guardian*, 28 August 1991, p. 6.

2. Facts and figures

1. A. Baker and S. Duncan, 'Child sexual abuse: a study of prevalence in Great Britain', *Child Abuse and Neglect* 9, 1985, p. 458.
2. M. Schecter and L. Roberge, 'Child sexual abuse' in R. Heller and C. Kempe, eds, *Child Abuse and Neglect: the Family and the Community* (Cambridge, MA: Ballinger, 1976), p. 60.
3. D. Glaser and S. Frosh, *Child Sexual Abuse* (London: BASW/Macmillan, 1988), p. 7.
4. ibid., pp. 9–12.
5. D. Finkelhor, 'Sexual abuse in a national survey of men and women', *Child Abuse and Neglect* 14, Spring 1990, pp. 19–28.
6. C. Nash and D. West, 'Victimisation of young girls', in D. West, ed, *Sexual Victimisation*, Aldershot: Gower, 1985.
7. See Baker and Duncan.
8. K. Pringle, *Managing to Survive: developing a resource for sexually abused young people* (Barnardo's North East, 1990), Appendix 2, p. 3.
9. Lord Justice Butler-Sloss, *Report of the Inquiry into Child Sexual Abuse in Cleveland 1987* (London: HMSO, 1988), p. 275.
10. S. Viinikka, 'Child sexual abuse and the law', in E. Driver and A.

Droisen, eds, *Child Sexual Abuse: Feminist Perspectives* (London: Macmillan, 1989), p. 149.

11. J. Clark, 'The price of innocent experience', *The Guardian*, 13 February 1990, p. 23.

12. R. P. Arnold, D. Rogers and D. A. G. Cook, 'Medical problems of adults who were sexually abused in childhood', *British Medical Journal* 300, 1990, p. 705.

13. Glaser and Frosh, p. 9.

14. Pringle, Appendix 2, p. 11.

15. ibid.

16. L. Kelly, L. Regan and S. Burton, 'An exploratory study of the prevalence of sexual abuse in a sample of 1200 16- to 21-year-olds', *Final Report to the ESRC*, Polytechnic of North London, 1991.

17. M. Elliott, 'Women who sexually abuse children: the last taboo', *Kidscape: First National Conference on Female Sexual Abusers*, Kidscape, 1992.

18. A. Borrowdale, *Distorted Images* (London: SPCK, 1991), p. 112.

19. Pringle, Appendix 2, p. 15.

20. L. Kelly, article in 'Inside' supplement to *Community Care*, 25 June 1992, pp. i–ii.

21. C. Dey and B. Print, 'Young children who exhibit sexually abusive behaviour' in A. Bannister, ed., *From Hearing to Healing: Working with the Aftermath of Child Sexual Abuse*, London: Longmans, 1992.

22. P. Parks, *Rescuing the Inner Child* (London: Souvenir Press, 1990), p. 31.

23. S. Wolf, *Evaluation and Treatment of the Sexual Offender*, Seattle: Sexual Assault Center, 1984.

24. J. V. Becker and J. A. Hunter, 'Evaluation of treatment outcome for adult perpetrators of child sexual abuse', *Criminal Justice and Behavior*, 19, March 1992, pp. 74–92.

25. *Evening Gazette*, Middlesbrough, 4 April 1992, p. 1.

26. J. Ogden, 'Rigorous exercise', *Social Work Today* 24:5, 24 September 1992, p. 25.

27. R. Marchant, 'Myths and facts about sexual abuse and children with disabilities', *Child Abuse Review* 5:2, Summer 1991, pp. 22–4.

28. P. Sullivan and J. Scanlan, 'Psychotherapy with handicapped sexually abused children', *Developmental Disabilities Bulletin* 18:2, 1991, pp. 21–34.

29. M. Hendessi, *4 in 10: Report on Young Women Made Homeless as a result of Child Sexual Abuse*, London: CHAR, 1992.

30. Department of Health and Social Security, *Diagnosis of Child Sexual Abuse: Guidance for Doctors* (London: HMSO, 1988), p. 8.

31. R. Butman, quoted in M. Kennedy, 'Christianity – help or hindrance for the abused child?', *Child Abuse Review* 5:3, Winter 1991/2, p. 3.

3. Responses

1. D. B. Allender, *The Wounded Heart*, Farnham: CWR, 1991.
2. ibid, p. 31.
3. ibid, pp. 19–20.
4. ibid, p. 41.
5. ibid, pp. 14–15.
6. M. Hendessi, *4 in 10: Report on Young Women who Become Homeless as a result of sexual abuse in childhood* (London: CHAR, 1992), p. 70.
7. J. Robertson, *Abuse Within the Family* (Bath: Creative Publishing, 1987), p. 100.
8. Lord Justice Butler-Sloss, *Report of the Inquiry into Child Abuse in Cleveland 1987* (London: HMSO, 1988), p. 161.
9. ibid.
10. L. Bennetts, 'Unholy Acts', *Vanity Fair* 54:12, December 1991, pp. 130–5, 166–71.
11. ibid, p. 132.
12. ibid, p. 133.
13. S. Rossetti, *Slayer of the Soul* (Mystic, CN: Twenty-Third Publications, 1991), p. 159.
14. *The Guardian*, 20 July 1990, p. 10.
15. Canadian Conference of Catholic Bishops, *From Pain to Hope*, Conacan Inc., 1992.
16. BBC 1, *Everyman*,'Breach of Faith', 23 May 1993.
17. BBC, *Look North*, 11 June 1993.

4. 'Crawling along a rough and painful road'

1. S. Shaw, 'Breaking the cycle', *New Internationalist*, September 1988, p. 25.
2. S. Richardson and H. Bacon, eds, *Child Sexual Abuse: Whose Problem? – Reflections from Cleveland*, (Birmingham: Venture Press, 1991), p. 72.
3. C. Doyle, *Working with Abused Children* (London: BASW/ Macmillan, 1990), p. 34.
4. A. Alvarez, lecture in South Cleveland Hospital, Middlesbrough, 13 March 1992.
5. T. Hansen, *Adult Survivors of Child Sexual Abuse: Some Guidelines for First Disclosure*, privately published, 1992.
6. M. M. Fortune, *Violence in the Family: a Workshop Curriculum for Clergy and Other Helpers* (Cleveland, OH: Pilgrim Press, 1991), p. 82.
7. D. Walsh and R. Liddy, *Surviving Sexual Abuse* (Dublin: Attic Press, 1989), pp. 27–8.
8. T. Hansen, *Seven for a Secret* (London: SPCK/Triangle, 1991), p. 3.
9. T. Hansen, 'Healing the Wound of Sexual Abuse', *The Tablet*, 2 June 1990, pp. 698–9.
10. Hansen, *Seven for a Secret*, p. 105.
11. P. Trible, *Texts of Terror*, Philadelphia: Fortress, 1984.
12. M. Kennedy, *Stations of the Cross*, unpublished.

13. E. Bass and L. Davis, *The Courage to Heal* (New York: Harper & Row, 1988), p. 120.
14. Hansen, 'Healing the Wound of Sexual Abuse'.
15. A. Campbell, *The Gospel of Anger* (London: SPCK, 1986), p. 102.
16. A. Imbens and I. Jonker, *Christianity and Incest* (Tunbridge Wells: Burns & Oates, 1992), p. 209.
17. J. N. Poling, *The Abuse of Power: a Theological Problem* (Nashville, TN: Abingdon, 1991), p. 40.
18. Imbens and Jonker, p. 164.
19. ibid, p. 39.
20. J. C. Brown and R. Parker, 'For God so Loved the World?' in J. C. Brown and C. R. Bohn, eds, *Christianity, Patriarchy and Abuse* (New York: Pilgrim Press, 1990), p. 9.
21. ibid.
22. Hansen, *Seven for a Secret*, p. 113.
23. J. Robertson, *Abuse Within the Family* (Bath: Creative Publishing, 1987), p. 97.
24. M. Pellauer, ed., *Sexual Assault and Abuse: a Handbook for Clergy and Religious Professionals* (New York: HarperCollins, 1991), p. 82.
25. ibid, pp. 82–3.
26. Fortune, *Violence in the Family*, p. 177.
27. Kennedy, 'Christianity-help or hindrance for the abused child?', p. 3.
28. Pellauer, *Sexual Assault*, p. 71.
29. M. M. Fortune and F. Wood, 'The Center for the Prevention of Sexual and Domestic Violence: a Study in Applied Feminist Theology and Ethics', *Journal of Feminist Studies in Religion* 4:1, Spring 1988, pp. 115–22.
30. Bass and Davis, *The Courage to Heal*, p. 156.

5. The war against children

1. D. Hechler, *The Battle and the Backlash* (Lexington, MA: Lexington Books, 1988), pp. 152–3.
2. D. Hechler, *The Battle and the Backlash* (Lexington, MA: Lexington Books, 1988), pp. 118–29.
3. J. Prosser, *Child Abuse Investigations: the Families' Perspective*, PAIN, 1992.
4. M. Midgley, *Wickedness*, London: Routledge and Kegan Paul, 1984.
5. M. Bavidge, *Mad or Bad?*, Bristol: Bristol Classical Press, 1989.
6. Midgley, p. 70.
7. Bavidge, p. 4.
8. His Honour Judge Pigot, *Report of the Advisory Group on Video Evidence*, London: Home Office, 1989.
9. J. La Fontaine, *Child Sexual Abuse* (Oxford: Polity Press, 1990), p. 10.
10. A. Miller, *For Your Own Good: the Roots of Violence in Child-rearing* (London: Virago, 1987), p. 283.

6. Ritual abuse

1. T. Tate, *Children for the Devil: Ritual Abuse and Satanic Crime*, London: Methuen, 1991.
2. P. Bibby, book review, *Social Work Today* 23:3, 12 September 1991, p. 18.
3. B. Campbell, paper given at a conference on ritual abuse, Polytechnic of North London, 13 December 1991.
4. ibid.
5. Tate, pp. 340–1.
6. 'Convicted paedophile jailed for killing and raping boy of 7', *The Times*, 23 October 1992, p. 3.
7. 'Slaughter of the lambs', *Sunday Times*, 23 June 1991, p. 9.

7. Where do we go from here?

1. S. Rossetti, *Slayer of the Soul*, Mystic, CN: Twenty-Third Publications, 1991.
2. A. J. Placa, 'Legal Aspects of the Sexual Abuse of Children', in Rossetti, p. 167.
3. Personal communication.
4. C. Bagley and K. King, *Child Sexual Abuse: the Search for Healing* (London: Routledge, 1990), p. 203.
5. J. N. Poling, *The Abuse of Power: a Theological Problem* (Nashville, TN: Abingdon, 1991), p. 121.
6. R. Quintanilla, in *Vocation for Justice* 5:3, Autumn 1991, p. 3.
7. Norma, in *Safety Net*, 1, no date.

Further reading

Child sexual abuse

Bagley, C. and King, K., *Child Sexual Abuse: the Search for Healing*. London: Routledge, 1990.

Bannister, A., ed., *From Hearing to Healing*. London: Longman, 1992.

Bentovim, A., *Child Sexual Abuse Within the Family: Assessment and Treatment*. London: Butterworth, 1988.

Doyle, C., *Working with Abused Children*. London: BASW/Macmillan, 1990.

Glaser, D. and Frosh, S., *Child Sexual Abuse*. London: BASW/Macmillan, 1988.

La Fontaine, J., *Child Sexual Abuse*. Oxford: Polity Press, 1990.

Richardson, S. and Bacon, H., eds, *Child Abuse: Whose Problem? – Reflections from Cleveland*. Birmingham: Venture Press, 1991.

Child sexual abuse and Christianity

Brown, J. C. and Bohn, C. R., *Christianity, Patriarchy and Abuse*. New York, Pilgrim Press, 1990.

Gibbs, P., *Child Sexual Abuse: a Concern for the Church?* Bramcote: Grove, 1992.

Hansen, T., *Seven for a Secret*. London, SPCK/Triangle, 1991.

Imbens, A. and Jonker, I., *Christianity and Incest*. Tunbridge Wells: Burns & Oates, 1992.

Pellauer, M., ed., *Sexual Assault and Abuse: a Handbook for Clergy and Religious Professionals*. New York: HarperCollins, 1987.

Poling, J., *The Abuse of Power: a Theological Problem*. Nashville, TN: Abingdon, 1991.

Rossetti, S., *Slayer of the Soul: Child Sexual Abuse and the Catholic Church*. Mystic, CN: Twenty-Third Publications, 1990.

For abuse survivors

Bain, O. and Sanders, M., *Out in the Open: a Guide for Young People who have been Sexually Abused*. London: Virago, 1990.

Bass, E. and Davis, L., *The Courage to Heal*. New York: Harper & Row, 1988.

Hall, L. and Loyd, S., *Surviving Child Sexual Abuse*. London: Falmer Press, 1989.

Keene, J. E., *A Winter's Song: a Litany for Women Seeking Healing from Childhood Sexual Abuse*. New York: Pilgrim Press, 1991.

Lew, M., *Victims no Longer: Men Recovering from Incest and other Child Sexual Abuse*. New York: Harper & Row, 1990.
Walsh, D. and Liddy, R., *Surviving Child Sexual Abuse*. Dublin: Attic Press, 1980.

Training resources
Armstrong, H., *Taking Care: a Church Response to Children, Adults and Abuse*. London: National Children's Bureau, 1991.
Fortune, M., *Violence in the Family: a Workshop Curriculum for Clergy and Other Helpers*, Cleveland, OH: Pilgrim Press, 1991.

Sources of help

For abused children
National Society for the Prevention of Cruelty to Children
Child Protection Helpline 0800 800 500
Local NSPCC offices can be found in the local phone directory.

Childline
Tel. 0800 1111
or write to Freepost 1111, London N1 0BR.

Childline (Scotland)
Tel. 041–552 1123

National Children's Home
85 Highbury Park Road
London N5 1UD
Tel. 071–226 2033
(The NCH has eleven treatment centres in the UK for abused children.)

Childwatch
206 Hessle Road
Hull
North Humberside HU3 3BH
Tel. 0482–25552

For Survivors
Most Rape Crisis Centres now offer counselling for women survivors of csa. Local Rape Crisis Centres are listed in the telephone directory. Among the largest are:

London Rape Crisis Line
P.O. Box 69
London WC1X 9NJ
Tel. 071–837 1600

Manchester Rape Crisis
P.O. Box 336
Manchester M60 2BS
Tel. 061–834 8784

Leeds Rape Crisis
P.O. Box 27
Leeds LS2 7EG
Tel. 0532–440058

Liverpool Rape Crisis
P.O. Box 64
Liverpool L69 8AP
Tel. 051–727 7599

Edinburgh Rape Crisis
P.O. Box 120
Head P.O., Brunswick Road
Edinburgh EH1 3ND
Tel. 031–556 9437

Bangor Rape Crisis Line
Abbey Road Centre
Bangor
Gwynedd LL57 2EA
Tel. 0428–354885

Belfast Rape Crisis Centre
P.O. Box 46
Belfast BT2 7AR
Tel. 0232–249696

Other helping resources include:

Rape and Sexual Abuse Support Centre
P.O. Box 908
London SE25 5EL
Tel. 081–688 0332

Shanti
1a Dalbury House
Edmondbury Court
Ferndale Road
London SW9 8AP
Tel. 071–733 8581

Incest and Sexual Abuse Support
85 Millgate
Newark on Trent
Notts NG24 4UA
Tel. 0636–610313

Women's Therapy Centre
6 Manor Gardens
London N7 6LA
Tel. 071–263 6200

Women and Medical Practice
40 Turnpike Lane
London N8 OPS
Tel. 081–888 2782

Christian Survivors of Sexual Abuse
c/o St John the Baptist Church
3 King Edward's Road
Hackney
London E9

Safety Net
c/o St George's Hospital
Tooting
London SW17

For black and ethnic minority women

Southall Black Sisters
52 Norwood Road
Southall
Middlesex
Tel. 081–571 9595

Muslim Women's Helpline
Tel. 071–700 2507/2509

Lambeth Women and Children Health Project
407 Wandsworth Road
London SW8 2JQ
Tel. 071–737 7151

Young Asian Women's Project
6–9 Manor Gardens
London N7 6LA
Tel. 071–272 4231

Subah
P.O. Box 30
JEDO
Manchester M12 4LL

For men

Survivors
P.O. Box 2470
London W2 1NW
Tel. 071–833 3737

Post-Survivors Group for Men
c/o Fighting Back
P.O. Box 1968
London N8 7AW

Project for men who have been sexually abused
Off Centre
25 Hackney Grove
London E8
Tel. 081–986 4016

MOVE (Men Overcoming Violence)
c/o Friends Meeting House
6 Mount Street
Manchester M1
Tel. 061–226 1216

For survivors of ritual abuse

Beacon Foundation
3 Grosvenor Avenue
Rhyll
Clwyd LL18 4HA
Tel. 0745–343600

SAFE
23 Highfield Road
Amesbury
Wiltshire SP4 7HX
Tel. 0980–623137

For people with learning difficulties who have been sexually abused

RESPOND
c/o 89 Ashurst Drive
Barkingside
Ilford
Essex IG6 1EW
Tel. 0483–418075

For deaf people who have been sexually abused
Keep Deaf Children Safe
Nuffield Hearing and Speech Centre
325 Gray's Inn Road
London WC1X 0DA
Tel. Margaret Kennedy 071–833 5627

For mothers of abused children
Mothers of Abused Children
25 Warnpool Street
Silloth
Cumbria
Tel. 06973–31432

MOSAC (Mothers of Sexually Abused Children)
P.O. Box 1008
Edinburgh EH8 7TH

Saheli (for Asian mothers)
Tel. 061–225 5111/9293

Refuges and housing for young women escaping from sexual abuse
CHOICES (Cambridge House for Incest Survivors)
7c Station Road
Cambridge CB1 2JB
Tel. 0223–314438/467897

1 in 4 Project
c/o Bradford Resource Centre
31 Manor Row
Bradford BD1 4PS
Tel. 0274–305276

Washington Women in Need
1st Floor, The Elms
Concord
Washington NE37 2BA
Tel. 091–416 3550

For abusers
Everyman
30a Brixton Road
Kennington
London SW9 6BU
Tel. 071–793 0155

Gracewell Clinic
Clinic Manager
25–29 Park Road
Moseley
Birmingham B13 8AH
Tel. 021–442 4994

For families of abusers
Aftermath
P.O. Box 414
Sheffield S1 3UP

Someone Cares
CVS Self-Help Project
MEA House
Ellison Place
Newcastle-upon-Tyne NE1 8XS
Tel. 091–232 7445

Community action
CAUSE (Cleveland Against Child Abuse)
c/o 37 Station Road
Norton
Cleveland TS20 1NH
Tel. 0642–559327

Justice for Abused Children
16 Woodbine Avenue
Gosforth
Newcastle-upon-Tyne NE3 4EU
Tel. 091–285 1258

Index